The
Business
God

Never Trust But Show

THE BUSINESS GOD

Never Trust but Show

SHIVAM JAYASWAL

Publisher

Krishna Computer Sansthan

Prayagraj

ISBN : 978-81-953793-5-4

Publisher
Krishna Computer Sansthan
63/59, Mori, Daraganj, Prayagraj 211006
+91-9450407739
Email : krishnacomputersansthan@gmail.com

First Edition : 2021

Go through my inspirational and motivational blogs on self-transformation and personal development ...
https://self-transformation-of-life.blogspot.com/?m=1

Book Receiving Address
Shivam Jayaswal
Sarvodaya Nagar, Bharadwaj Puram
Prayagraj – 211006

Page Setting
Brahmanand Mishra

Printed by :
Infinity Imaging Systems
New Delhi

Dedicated to

My grandfather

With deepest reverence

And to

My mother and my father

Whose life is the embodiment of constant struggle, which teach me the lesson of never give up.

Prologue

Money and power are given the most importance in this world and there is no greater curse than poverty. A bitter truth of history, the world is ruled by the one who has the largest treasure of wealth.

So two great stock investor of their time combat to get the same treasure of wealth and hundreds of people are burnt to ashes in the blaxe of their obstinacy.

A mantra for business, 'Act like you trust people, but don't', all the characters in this book know very well but despite this, such a mirage is prepared by The Business God in which a great stock investor of India of his own time get trapped in an accusation and he is accused that he has done terror funding in the train bomb blast of July 2011 of Mumbai, so that he can earn lots of money through short selling by crashing the stock market.

The Business God was that person who in a jiffy could create a monopoly of any businessman of his field of industry; in return, he would take from them a lot of money. But no one knows his real name.

When a middle class person walks on straight paths, stepped into the outer world with immense intelligence, the nepotism and favoritism of that time took away his dream. And then in that poverty when he saw his father dying of cancer, that incident destroyed all the good in him; and he realized that it was only necessary to earn money, whether that path is right or wrong doesn't matter. And he vowed that one day he would make all those to bow down at his feet, who had insulted him.

And no one even thought that this favoritism and nepotism would make a business consultant, 'The Business God'.

Many agencies like RAW and CBI couldn't catch him till date because he used to destroy all the evidence with perfection. Even those businessmen, who have seen him, were afraid to take the name of Business God in front of the police.

There is rivalry between two businessmen, Gajendra Rai and Samrat Singh 'Sikandar' for only reason that is they want to gain power and remain in power.

Samrat Singh 'Sikandar' who grew up in an orphanage and understood the ponderosity of poverty and understood that a poor person is like a living corpse who has no respect in society and even his own family members don't respect him so he took a vow that he didn't want to live such a life again, that's why he sets out on the path of becoming rich by wrong means. And gradually, he put his insiders in every small and big company of India and in every stock firm of Mumbai; from whom he gets all the inside information of any company, which is of course an illegal method of trading in stocks, and when he got that then he would earns crores of rupees by investing in those stocks or by shorting.

When Samrat was young, so cleverly he spellbound a very great investor, Rudra Pratap Singh, the owner of Singh Broking Solutions, with his intellect, due to which he adopted him and gave half of his legacy to him.

The remaining half of the legacy belonged to Indra Singh, the real son of Rudra Pratap Singh; and because of this split, Indra Singh became a sworn enemy of Samrat.

Rudra Pratap Singh had made such a will before his death that if one of his two sons does business through wrong means, then all his inheritance will be transferred to the another son, but if either of these two dies, that property will go to charity; for this reason, Indra chose the path of exposing the wrongdoings of Samrat, not to kill Samrat. For which he went to Gajendra Rai to ask for help.

Gajendra Rai, the owner of Rai Securities Limited, was also a royal blood and on his head was the crown of 'Stock Market King'. And due to this, Samrat determined to destroy him; for which he first befriended Gajendra and then taking advantage of his weakness, Samrat squandered a lot of his money.

After this, Indra reaches out to him by taking all the evidence so that he can convince him that Samrat is behind his loss. And then they two become friends and get involved in conspiracies to bring down Samrat's empire.

And they go to ask help form The Business God and then a battle begins

If you want the crown of flowers, all the thorns have to be removed and this story is about dislodging those thorns that's how a businessman goes to any extent to ruin his rival.

Every human being in this world is selfish and engaged in fulfilling his own selfishness; he first wins the trust of others and when he achieves his purpose, then he put a dagger in their back.

And then The Business God hatches a plot to trap a con, Samrat Singh 'Sikandar'.

He first finds anyhow the weakness of Samrat and then turns his most trusted man by his side.

"In statesmanship no one is an enemy forever and no one is friend forever, only realization of our selfish interest, sometimes by enmity and sometimes by friendship."

- The Business God

And then in this rivalry, hundreds of people fall prey to that train bombings.

Introduction

This book highlights the importance of power and money, a rich person may say that money does not bring happiness, but for a hungry poor, true happiness resides at only two square meals which can be achieved only and only by money. If there is one thing that is most worshiped after God in this world, it is money.

In this world people respect only those who have money, the more money he has, the more respect he has in the society.

There has never been a bigger law court than history and the decision of history has always been with the powerful side. We have to fight a battle at every turn of life and the one who wins the battle is the one who is powerful in every dimension and then he could change the pages of history according to himself so that future generations will only worship him. Alexander is also called 'The Great' because he was powerful.

This book is also about some of those powerful personalities who have changed history from time to time according to them. However, all the characters in this book are fictional. But the fact can't be turned away from that no one is ever belongs to anyone in the business industry; here everyone can harm anyone for their own benefit. A character Samrat Singh 'Sikandar' in this book kills his father for fear of losing the legacy and his step-brother Indra Singh, in grief of losing half of that legacy, kills his own father.

In the greed of getting an undisputed sway in stock market, Samrat Singh 'Sikandar', Gajendra Rai and Indra Singh are ready to make the bloodbath of hundreds in which The Business God has an important role.

The quasi-royal ruler of business industry is The Business God whose evil eye makes all the businessmen tremble with fear and no intelligence agency ever caught him; and this man has unshakable faith in the complete suppression of the enemy. He uses 'Trust' as a double-edged sword and as the story ends, the lesson is taught that no one in the world is worthy of trust, but for the fulfilment of selfish interest, it is necessary to win the loyalty of the people by expressing love and always assure them that you trust them.

This book has been composed after one year of hard work to present the sum and substance of credos of life and success, the person who read it can never be deceived by anyone in life and no one can ever dominate him. Many thrilling incidents like insider trading, short selling, metamorphic virus attack on telecom servers, terrorist attack have been narrated in this book which enchant and stun the reader at every turn. The ambushes between stock investors and The Business God described in the novel are reminiscent of the political maneuvers between Chanakya and Rakshas, described in Vishakhadatta's 'MUDRARAKSHAS'. Curiosity, novelty and wonder predominate in the presented object which staggered and astound the readers.

However, all the events in the book are fictional except the Mumbai train bombings of 2006; I just used facts to make the story thrilling from my point of view.

My thanks to the publisher Mr. Brahmanand Mishra, Krishna Computer Sansthan, 63/59, Mori, Daraganj, Prayagraj for intensive editing work on the manuscript.

And my special thanks to my grandfather Mr. Ram Kr. Jayaswal, Retd. Correspondence Officer (U.P. Education Deptt.), for his thoughtfulness in suggesting me the subtitle of the book, he always supports me in every turn of my life and shaped me to fight with this world.

I also want to show my gratitude to my parents Mr Surendra Kr. Jayaswal, Mrs Sushma Jayaswal and my younger sister Miss Shiwangi Jayaswal for always trusting me and supporting me in my every decision.

July 22, 2021   - Shivam Jayaswal

Index

Prologue.................................*vii*

Introduction.............................*xi*

One................................ 01-18

Two...............................19-53

Three 54-62

Four 63-82

Five 83-91

Six 92-104

Seven 105-120

Eight 121-131

Nine 132-146

Ten 147-167

Eleven.........................168-200

Twelve 201-224

ONE

"The whole world knows that without God's will, not a single leaf is moved in the same way nothing happens in the industry without the will of The Business God"

- The Business God

Software engineer hurriedly entered in the cabin-"Sir, there is huge problem in our servers."

"So what happened, go get on the backup servers and call the technicians"-Supervisor said with a smile.

"Sir, our backups are also not working.

I think there is a virus inside our servers"-Engineer was covered in sweat.

"What the non-sense are you saying"-Supervisor stood up and went up toward servers room-"Have you any idea, what it means?"

February 22, 2006, Mumbai;

In Mobile Switching Center of a telecommunication company AIRCEIL, a famous company which have 16.07 million subscribers in December 2008, 7th biggest telecom operator of INDIA at its own time.

The task of an MSC (Mobile switching center) is to connect one's call to another person whom that person wants to talk. There is lot of responsibilities in switching center of every network provider. They also transfer SMS and FAX to the right person. In these servers, all confidential details of their subscribers are stored.

Entering in the server's room, that supervisor loudly asked–"Why our servers are not working?"

"We think there is a dangerous computer virus in servers"–A software engineer reported from the other side of that server room.

"Which type of virus?"

"Sir, our anti-virus system failed to decrypt that malicious code so we think it must be type of metamorphic codes.

"What?"–Supervisor astonished–"How is it possible? Who could do this because strangers are not allowed in MSC?

And our technicians are..."–Supervisor stopped because there must be hands of any insider of MSC.

But now what he could do.

He called on his superior boss and told him all disruptions and he gets horror-strucked when he get knew that same problem is also happened in two other MSCs of AIRCEIL.

The MSC of AIRCEIL in Kolkata and Chennai is already collapsed and technicians are failed to decrypt the malicious code.

Who could do this and why? What he would get from this?

One software engineer in every MSC is on leave today and no one is able to connect with them. Maybe they have done it only. But from where will such a dangerous virus come to them; because no one can easily achieve Metamorphic Engine. Common viruses, after infecting the files, they modify their decryption module (the program of conversion of encrypted data into its original form) slightly so that no anti-virus can detect that code but in metamorphic codes, they modify their decryption module totally, they don't leave any clue of pattern of changing codes, hence it is very difficult to decrypt that type of metamorphic codes. This is the reason why technicians are failed to make anti-virus program for this virus.

Moreover, they were preparing to such an extent that the virus was also put in the backup servers.

Every MSC supervisor has received orders from above that this news should not be leaked out.

But who is that dangerous organization, who has that much money to afford metamorphic engine? Were all those missing software engineers already members of that organization? How did they target 3 MSCs at the same time? And how long will the fourth MSC be able to remain safe?

Many questions...but no one is able to answer...

Who have taken responsibility for this service, they get locked themselves in meeting room. All board members are silence tight. They are not facing media because what they will say, they don't know.

India doesn't know what is wrong with the AIRCEIL network, matter of network issue in AIRCEIL is buzzing around all over the country. But what is the reality behind this, no one knows.

In meeting room, the fog of terror is becoming dense because they know the data of subscribers is also being lost. And when this news will be leak out, the reputation of company will be totally down-and-out. And it is sure to go to jail. But what they do, they do not understand anything.

They are bewildered.

Gradually, AIRCEIL is losing its subscribers. They are being abused from all over the country. But they are helpless; because that technology has not yet been made that can decrypt it. And it is impossible for that technology into existence so soon.

So far, it has been badly affected by the company's reputation which can be gauged from the down fall in its share price. And as the anger of the people increases, the share price of the company is decreasing in the same proportion. Don't know what will happen when the news of this virus comes out? People will take off the skins to flay of the owners of the company when they come to know that their personal information has gone into the hands of a thief.

Today, the company had lost 6.62% before the market was closed. Now do not know how much will be opened tomorrow? Short sellers have become active. And those people will take full advantage of it.

Due to no official statement from the company, the pressure on them is constantly increasing, but they do not know what to do? Because the lie told will not last long and speaking the truth, the company's share price will fall below the setback due to which the company will have to bear the loss of billions of rupees. And where will the company fall due to this virus, no one knows anything.

The company's competitors are happy that their competition is decreasing. But even the competitors have not been able to find out the real reason behind it.

How long will the remaining one MSC of AIRCEIL be able to bear the load? Do not know how many subscribers' information has been infected.

Troubled customers are spreading negative comments about the company on social media. Through social media, this chain continues to grow. Gradually, big personalities are spreading their anger toward the company through social media and now even this issue has become a hot topic for digital media. Discussions of AIRCEIL's poor network service are being discussed on every news channel.

Due to this reason, the stock value of this company was already reduced from Rs. 72.52 to Rs. 67.72 but now the next day, not knowing how much share will be open, nothing can be said about it but it is certain that there will be a Gap-down opening (If the share price opens at a price lower than previous day's closing price, it is known as gap down opening) because the negativity spreads like a forest fire. What comes in its grip remains scorched, where will fire of negativity ends and when will it ends, hard to guess.

The people of the authority of the AIRCEIL Company are constantly in contact with those technicians who are engaged in breaking the virus.

Employees of every MSC have been imprisoned in that server rooms. But if this thing was hidden from the people for a long time, then what are the dreadful consequences of this, thinking that the major holding partner's sweat is being exempted. Some people associated with the management of the company are repeatedly singing the technical issue with their social media handle but nobody is paying attention to their words. The whole of India is waiting for this urgent Board meeting to end because after this, they will come to the press and explain the exact reason behind this bad service.

It is the 8 o'clock in the evening. The media crowd outside the office is increasing and the company's negative commentary barrage is not stopping on social media platforms.   Many stock experts are advising to sell AIRCEIL's stock. #sellAirceil is on trend everywhere on the blogging websites. But at the same time, everyone also knows that AIRCEIL is such a prestigious company that its years of fame cannot be buried in the ground in a single day. And this is the reason that more than half of the people of India are waiting for the official statement of the company but those who will give that statement have locked themselves in a hall and are praying that soon the virus matter is sorted out. But this thing is not in their hands. These people cannot even go to the people because the whole of INDIA is eyeing to them. And people are waiting that if they get know the secret behind this deteriorated service of AIRCEIL, then they could sell the company's stock. Everyone is sure that the Gap-down opening must have fallen somewhere, breaking all the Supports (It is the price level which prevents the price from declining further). RII (Retail investor individual) has sold its huge amount of share of AIRCEIL under AMO (After market order).

Do not know which trouble has come at all. This day is the black day in the history of AIRCEIL Company. Everyone is praying that this disaster should be averted soon.

This is the work of a dangerous mind of a dangerous human being but who knows what that person is?

It's 09:15 pm, Anchor of NDTV Profit, an Indian news TV channel, comes and says- "People of India, hold your breath because listening to what we are going to tell you, you are all scared out of your wits. We will give you an answer to that question in a while, the answer to which all the people of India want to know from this afternoon.

After all, what is the reason that the service of a reputed telecom company AIRCEIL suddenly deteriorated? Who is behind all this, who took away the pleasure of the owners of AIRCEIL?"

The anchor carries a CD in his hands, in which

written 'REASON BEHIND THE FALL OF AIRCEIL'. Showing that CD on TV he said–"I want to tell the people of India that right now at 09:00 pm someone has sent this CD to our office. The envelope containing this CD had only one line written in it and that was an identity. Yes, this is the name that half of the people of India have heard but no one has seen that person till date and it is not just a name but a creepy brand behind whom CBI, RAW like agencies are pursuing relentlessly but till date nobody has caught him.

This is the name that people bow down in fear after hearing it. No one dares to speak openly against this man. And he is the one to sets all the industries to dance at his tune, 'THE BUSINESS GOD'."

Half of India has stopped right there on hearing this, surprised wonder is visible on everyone's face. All eyes are on the same TV channel. Everyone has stopped their work. Because there were many people who had heard the stories of 'THE BUSINESS GOD', so many get mordant by this name, so many found this name full of curiosity. Many things were prevalent about the Business God, some believed it, and some take it as absurd things. Nobody talks about him openly. People had seen an example of this, a few years ago, one person had spoken a lot of abuses by targeting 'The Business God', that businessman went bankrupt within one year. His personal and professional life was ruined, that person is still alive today, but seems like his existence has been disappeared from the society. People have since never tagged Business God in any of their speeches on any platform. Those who have heard this name and believed in it, they understood that this time The Business God has come to frighten the whole of India with his style. He wants to hear the noise of the name of 'The Business God' all over India.

Some people still not believing this but the worst is

the condition of those board members. Dead silence to prevail in Board meeting room. All of them are eyeing the same news channel. And all of them were also well acquainted with the style of The Business God. Those people understood that if Business God has a hand in ruining them, they can do nothing no matter how much they implore in front of him. There will only happen what The Business God wants but the biggest fear of all of this of the news of virus attack to go public, otherwise the company's reputation to be ruined today.

Today, more than half of India is watching NDTV Profit news TV channel, its TRP reached the top in all other news channel. And they will get a lot of benefit in future because of this. Now the name of the NDTV will be on tongue of every person who has invested in any company. Everyone is calling someone and asking to watch NDTV Profit. Millions of viewers are added to the NDTV channel in a 5-minute break which has broken all the records so far.

The break ends and the same news anchor comes in front-"Those who are not aware do not get the truth, that's why always watch NDTV to be aware.

So, I was telling the people of India, who is behind the plight of the AIRCEIL company. That is the hands of The Business God. Yes, this is The Business God who ruled this unbridled industry like an Emperor. The whole of India knows that in the business industry everything happens at the will of The Business God. And now I am going to play that audio which when we heard, we all got scared. And I want to present that audio to the whole of India."

That anchor sits silently after turning on the CD player.

The waves of the sea are breaking on the shore. Only the sound of the waves is heard. After a while, a person

that maybe The Business God says with a heavy voice-
"Every person sitting in power has a fear that the crown of his head may not be snatched away from him and I had to come to realize the kings of AIRCEIL that sip of bitter truth and bash of defeat is better for him as soon as he perceives.

The whole world knows that without God's will, not a single leaf is moved in the same way nothing happens in the industry without the will of The Business God.

When people start forgetting God, he has to do some miracles to remind them of his existence that's why I also had to come to remind you all of my existence.

Yes, I have put MANDMET VIRUS in the servers of AIRCEIL Telecom Company. To remind this world that Business God dictates the business industry. And this outbreak is not going to stop yet.

Only The Business God will resound everywhere. Some will call me God and some will call me devil. But what to do, this world has become vile.

And to rule this malevolent world, it is very important to be evil."

A horrific laugh is heard for some time.

The whole of India goes demented. Today only two words are echoing all over India, the first one is 'MANDMET' and the second is 'THE BUSINESS GOD'.

Major holding partners sitting in a board meeting get traumatized. They get stunned and lost for words.

Perhaps the truth has been told that *the sapience of a moneyless person is destroyed.* They lost their prudence.

Now they don't have the courage to come out and to say something. Media has got topic. Now every news channel is discussing only and only about the 'THE

BUSINESS GOD'. Everyone is enouncing his strength. Commotion is everywhere. Many social media sites are being crashed. The question on every person's tongue is what the hell 'MANDMET VIRUS' is?

A great calamity to befall on short term investors, they squandered their money.

Now to answer all these question, those board members will have to come out otherwise this enraged India can do anything.

Now these owners are going to flay. All board members are sitting despondent. Now the whole of India is going to be abusive.

These people call in all switching center and tell them that now everybody can go to their home only a few people will stay there with the technicians.

All board members come in front of media with police protection. There is a barrage of questions from the media. But all these are standing statuesquely like someone has hit a big slap on their credibility. What answer should be given so that their remaining dignity remains intact. These people tell the whole truth one by one in front of the media because they have no choice.

These official statements added terror of Business God in the hearts of people. Those who had been taking it as rubbish things till now have to believe completely.

There is an atmosphere of terror all over India. Everyone has the fear in their minds that Business God said that this outbreak is not going to stop yet, now what it means? Everyone is making prediction.

But only two people know about the future, either God or The Business God.

It is night, but it is difficult for small investors to sleep.

As expected, next day AIRCEIL shares touch the lower circuit and the Sensex and Nifty fall drastically.

A dangerous brand was behind this, 'THE BUSINESS GOD'. It was only with his voice that instilled terror in the hearts of the people. And what a dangerous thing this is, people start trembling thinking about this. As Business God said that 'THE BUSINESS GOD' will echo everywhere, proved absolutely right.

Today, only The Business God's discussions are being held on every newspaper, every news TV channel and every platform of social media. The name of The Business God is on the tongue of every person. Everyone is curious to know about him. After all what is the quality inside him, which has made him the God of the business industry. And the more one knows about him, the more afraid he becomes. But the fear of all this is something that was predicted by The Business God.

Many agencies like CBI, RAW have started looking for The Business God in their own way.

There is big panic in Dalal Street; many people became frantic to scuffle due to losing their money.

Slowly, the news of The Business God is spreading all over the world and also the outbreak of MANDMET VIRUS. By now, the AIRCEIL Company was identified with the top telecom company; today it has been identified with the MANDMET VIRUS.

But no politician and business man is talking about The Business God.

So far, many antivirus software companies have started breaking the virus. All these companies are trying to break this virus and to earn a name in the market. Everybody is looking for an opportunity in this calamity. Several antivirus companies have been able to show their power to different switching centers of AIRCEIL.

AIRCEIL's competitors are lauding themselves by coming to the media and condemning the management of AIRCEIL Company. Many AIRCEIL subscribers have ported their number to BSNL.

The next day everyone was in fear of what the next move of Business God would be? Now, don't know how he wants to scare the people of India. But it is certain that whatever he said, it must have some truth. But who knows, the dreadful future about which many kinds of doubts are arising in the minds of people, maybe it is going to happen today.

It is 11:00 AM, now the subscribers of the TATA INDICOM Company are having difficulty in talking on the phone. Those who had problems in the beginning, understood that maybe as the AIRCEIL Company was ruined, similarly, TATA INDICOM is on the verge of ruin. By 12:00 AM, it has reached to the people that TATA INDICOM's phone was also facing problems. Media have come to round up the board members of TATA INDICOM Company.

So half of India's people are eyeing the NDTV Profit news TV channel, traders are now afraid to invest money in several companies because this time people have realized a minacious personality very closely. Many brokerage firms are also advising to withdraw their money. But all of this is victim of emulation; they think the majority is right.

But gradually, this news has showing on all news TV channels that there is something wrong in the mobile switching centers of TATA INDICOM.

Now India is getting why The Business God said that this outbreak is not going to stop yet.

Everyone's eye were on NDTV Profit that at 01:30 in

the afternoon a news TV anchor comes out and tells that MANDMET virus has also been attacked in mobile switching center of TATA INDICOM company as it happened at the servers of the AIRCEIL company.

On hearing this, there was a stampede among the people of India. Some people have started withdrawing their money, so many subscribers of TATA INDICOM are trying to contact their family.

In half an hour, TATA INDICOM's stock has fallen down to 15.5% which is the biggest downfall ever seen. Its shares are selling in price of dirt cheap.

There is again a lot of disappointment in the market. India didn't emerge yet from the downfall of 2 days ago and another blow that was given by that dangerous monster The Business God. Today a large army of traders is cursing Business God.

Who is that bloody Business God who depauperated many traders to fulfill his ego. The day when he fell into the clutches of police, the whole country would like to see him hanged.

Because people are bearing very malice toward The Business God but no one has the courage to reveal that resentment. But these sparks will definitely form a blaxe someday. And it is difficult to conjecture how far this fiery flame will spread and who will get corrugate.

Now many traders are feeling that like AIRCEIL and TATA INDICOM are devastated, just like that all the telecom companies will be collapsed. Now traders have started withdrawing money from all the companies of the telecom sector. There has been a decline in the stock of many companies like RELIANCE, BHARTI TELE-VENTURES, and VODAFONE etc. ·

But who benefits from all this, only time will show

because the stock market is the market where the money goes from the account of impatient traders to a patient investor. And in today's world, there is very little patient is remained; this is the main reason that causes inflation in the stock market.

But what one can do, money is such a thing, which fear of being lost staggered the patient of a sound person. And as soon as the prudence of impatient person is destroyed, money slips like sand from his clutches.

4 days passed in no time; there is still a lot of disappointment in the stock market. The shares of AIRCEIL and TATA INDICOM have fallen very much. Short sellers became active from day one, they cause share price to fall further.

The rest of the switching centers are working properly so there is some possibility of their share price going up.

Technicians and IT companies from all over the world are working hard day and night to crack the virus codes. No one had encountered this type of metamorphic malicious code. Many virus authors and hackers were also consulted to break these codes but all of them also failed.

A week is elapsing, but no one is able to break the codes of this virus. The stock market has grown significantly in this one week. But the situation of the telecom sector has not improved much. Now this loss can only be overcome when someone can break out of this virus.

Now the situation is that on the news channel, there is less news of The Business God but more about the MANDMET virus. Due to such publicity of this virus, people are losing their trust from big IT companies. And due to this side effect, the value of the stock of these companies is gradually decreasing. As telecom sector lost its faith in the market, in the same way, IT companies are losing their trust. They are repeatedly assuring that they will soon make the antivirus of this virus.

Discussion of this virus is resounding so much that it seems it can defeat that dreaded 'I LOVE YOU' virus in publicity.

Special superintendence is taking in switching centers of AIRCEIL and TATA INDICOM that the programming of this virus should not go out of these servers otherwise do not know how much data will go into the evil hands.

When people have less information about something, they start making negative things about it and this rumor viz smoke without fire catches people's ear. And when people hear those rumors from everyone, they believe it to be true.

Then there is so much power in these rumors that it also affects the daily life of people and when it can have an impact on daily life, then how would the stock market remain untouched by it.

Traders, swing investors are now selling stock of IT companies in huge quantities which has a very bad effect on the Sensex and Nifty. These companies have now understood that if in a few days they are unable to decrypt that virus, then the people of India will start blaming them directly which can have a very bad impact on the reputation of the company.

Almost 12 days have passed since the people of India heard the voice of The Business God. Many people still doubt that there is a person named Business God or someone has made a lewd joke with us.

Time went by, 3 more days have passed and then a miracle happens. An IT company made an antivirus program which can decrypt all types of metamorphic codes. Name of that company is Techpro AV public ltd. And they have named the antivirus program, 'M-killer' (metamorphic malicious code killer). The specialty of which is that it can decrypt any type of complicated metamorphic codes. The servers, in which the IT Company inserted its antivirus program, started working properly.

As soon as in the media, the owner of this IT Company gave good news, the enthusiasm of traders and investors increased again toward the market. The market has gained momentum again; people are enthusiastically buying shares, especially of Techpro AV public ltd.

For this miraculous work of Techpro AV Company, the big giant tech companies are giving their contract to this IT Company.

Today, a large population is happy that the truth has won again this time; God has defeated the evil and hold high the head of truth.

While on one side the Techpro AV Company's shares are rising up, on other side shares of remaining IT companies are falling down. One legitimate reason for the collapse of the shares of the tech giant companies is that they were not the first to make antivirus programs.

The rest of these companies are surprised that no technicians from Techpro AV Company came to any MSCs for a single day and by staying outside, that people made its antivirus, after all, how can this be possible?

But in response, the owner of Techpro AV Company said in media that his company has been engaged in the project of decrypting any type of metamorphic code for the last several years. They were so closed to making that antivirus when they get to know that there is a virus attack in servers of AIRCEIL and TATA INDICOM and found out that it is a virus program of metamorphic code. Hearing these things, we increased our speed three times and finally, first of all, we came in front of this world with 'M-killer' antivirus program.

Now the name of Techpro AV Company has come on the highest of all IT software companies in India. In the business industry, when a company is able to give the best and unique solution to a burning problem, they capture the large market share in the same proportion. And in this case, only one company Techpro AV public ltd. has a solution then it is obvious that Techpro AV will have the largest market share in its field.

The days for earning money in the stock market returned again. *And when people start seeing money, so they do not remember the pain of the injuries they suffered.*

So, the name of The Business God is now being heard less by the people. All people's lives are coming back on track. But it is sure that people will never completely forget The Business God.

This name has now become such a pang that people do not want to remember the pain of such injury because as soon as they remember about that wound, the pain will increase.

The smartest person in the field of stock market is not the one who knows the time of investment in market but the one who knows when to short (It is a position, created when a trader sells a security/stock first with the intention of repurchasing it or covering it later at a lower price) in market.

Because in the second case a person books higher profit in a very short period of time. And that's why short sellers become the richest in recession time. But it is also true that they have to take more risk than that of traditional investing. But the scene after these risks is not less than any paradise.

But to go to heaven you have to die.

Therefore to add millions of rupees to your wealth in such a short time, you will have to take so much risk.

That is why only two people have become very rich in such a short time of crisis by taking too much risk. Because these people had short the stocks of many companies in the telecom sector at the right time. And they are Gajendra Rai and Indra Singh, they are very happy so much as if they get a buried treasure somewhere.

TWO

"In this world, the one who has more money, he has more power. And the society does not respect those who do not have money, even their own family. Bitter but this is the reality. Remember that no one will support you in your struggle but when you succeed, the whole world will come to congratulate you."

- Tony's grandpa

5 hours ago,

Scene of a private island in The Bahamas:

A 60-year-old man is basking in the sun in a yard of a stately villa; who bought this island ten years ago and settled with his family. He was compelled to escape his native country India. His family asked many times why they had to leave India, but he never gave answer to this question.

Seeing that flock of dolphins, he lost in his past; that past about which he has not told his family, his family asked him many times about the secret of his enormous wealth, but he always remained silent about that. And what's behind it, no one knows. Sitting in the armchair, he is just looking at the sky...

The voice of his grandson is heard from behind- "Grandpa, I have decided my future."

"Good, you are not like those people who blame destiny for their future"- grandpa said with a smile.

Tony sits in front-"I will never be like those chicken-hearted who have the mentality to become like others.

Such a polluted mentality leaves that person as just a part of the crowd, who neither can think right nor can take right decisions and can't protect himself from adverse winds at the right time. This emulation mentality does not give him a persuasive message, nor does it allow him to make appropriate decisions and to make lofty paradigm. And when they are not become successful, they start assigning fault to their fortune."

Tony and his Grandfather laughing out loud.

Grandpa said-"So, how do you want to shape your future?"

"I want to become a business tycoon."

He looks at his grandson with a little surprise.

Tony says again-"I have been thinking about this for 2 weeks. What kind of job should I do in which I get more money in less hard work. From which kind of work, I can get a lot of respect from people. By doing what kind of work, I will be considered a prestigious citizen of the society.

After so much brainstorming, suddenly one thing came to my mind that if I have come into this world, I will make a noise of my name that people will remember my name for next ten generation. And I decided that I will reach that high level of success where people will have to raise their head too high to see my throne.

Then I felt that there can be no better person in society than a businessman. I want complete financial freedom. I will not allow anyone to order me; I do not want that someone else get benefit of my hard work.

I want my name to be No. 1 in the field of business. I want that people respect me as a business tycoon."

He is beholding at his grandson with a smile on his set face-"A business tycoon..."

"Yes grandpa, I want to be the richest person of this planet.

The ever richest...

And since I have dreamed it, I'm very excited about this journey. It's gonna be very thrilling. I have found that the life of a businessman is very adventurous. This life gives millions time more pleasure than that of boring and servile 9-5 job. There is a lot of freedom when no one is going to dictate to you as a boss. You can do that work which is right from your perspective. There is risk, personality development, passion and of course failure is also in this journey and many times, such difficulties arise in front of us, which are obstinate to exterminate us. But after facing all these obstacles and winning over these difficulties, there is success. Such a success, where clamour of your name resounds all over the world. Such a success when there is respect for you in the hearts of the whole world. Such successes, in which people make you their ideal, read about you and want to be like you. Through that success you have power in your hands. You can do whatever you want."

Tony's eyes to light up with the imagination of his beautiful future.

Blessing his grandson he said-"May God do as you wish."

A smile to came to Tony's lips, then he said-"Oh yes, I wanted to ask you something, because of which I was looking for you at home since morning."

"And what is that?"

"That question is, how does a businessman think? How does he take any decision? How does he beat his opponent? How should be the attitude of a successful businessman?

And my biggest curiosity is who should be trusted in business?"

His grandpa seems like he is searching for a passion of business in his grandson. He said-"Now you want to know that whom to trust in business.

This question is the most difficult of all the other questions you have asked.

But I will definitely answer this to you, after all a future Business God is asking me this question."

Tony startled-"Business God? Who is this? I think I heard this name somewhere...

Oh yes, I had heard this word when I was doing research about the life of a businessman. There was mention that he was a very malevolent businessman.

Who was he? And what he used to do? I'm very eager to know about him."

Grandpa heaves a deep sigh and cast an expressive sight over his grandson-"So, you want to know about The Business God?

Okay, my son...

So let me tell you his story.

In which you will get the answer to all the question asked. And the answer to that question will also be found, which is the most difficult question, 'whom to trust in business?'

Are you ready?"

"Yes, I'm ready."

"So now I am going to tell you about the person

whose motto of life was 'work with perfection'; who used to complete all his work with perfection. When he was juvenile, he had purpose in life to become a very famous business consultant and marketing expert. His favorite game was chess and perhaps that is why tactics and dangerous conspiracies kept circulating in his mind all the time. He believed in extirpate his enemies. *He believed that when the whole world can fit in these two eyes, we should never dream small.* He considered himself the best. He did not make anyone his friend because he did not find any person who was of the level of his mind. Nobody was able to find out his weakness or maybe he didn't have any weakness either.

When he was completing his graduation, his companions greatly admired his intelligence. But they were also jealous of him. By the age of 20, he completed his graduation and he made his first step to the outer world. He belongs to a lower middle class family and his family had only his father except him. He loved his father very much. He promised his father that he would become a prominent business consultant on the strength of his own mind. He will give his father a luxurious life as every lower middle class boy promises his family. He told his father that they would have palatial villa on a private island. It will be a relaxed life in which there will be no grievance.

But in the decade of 1980's, nepotism and favoritism were given more importance in India. The outer world did not appreciate his mind. He struggled a lot but could not move forward without any major support. Gradually, he was getting fed up with these rulers. His financial condition was getting worse from day to day. He was then working on little wages. And many times it happens that there is not even transport money to go from his working place to his home. He was very angry at the monarchy of businessmen of this world. But how would he take out his anger. By slowly, the pang in his heart was growing that he would one day take his revenge on them all. Even if the world was unaware of this, he knew the strength of his mind well.

There was still goodness in his heart; he does not want to achieve his goal through wrong paths. But perhaps God had written a different story on the pages of his life and the day came when all the goodness in him was gone because he saw his father dying of cancer in front of him. But he was helpless, he could not do anything, he did not have enough money to cure cancer of his father. The father to whom he had promised a luxurious life, that father did not have any serenity even till his death.

Now one thing was clear in his mind that it is necessary to achieve the goal whether the path is right or wrong. *If you worry about the way, this world will not let you live. You should never do such pomp and show so that you would consider as a respectable person in the society. If you are rich enough in money then this society will spontaneously consider you as a respectable person. He now understood that this world is full of selfish humans, every human is crazy about making money only. If you want to earn money, than you have to play with these selfish humans which are already doing by the businessmen of today.*

He now had nothing to lose but the whole world to gain. He knew well that he needed a Godfather to earn more fame and vogue in business who can assay his talent. Then he set out in search of that Godfather.

And one day that quest was over, in 1995, when he was 35 years old; he got the support of a Godfather."

"Who was that person and why did he made 'The Business God'?"

"Nobody knew this thing, but from some of the books written by him, people make conjectures that his Godfather must have been a stock market fraudster."

"Well how The Business God looks like?"-Tony is getting curious about him.

His grandpa smiles lightly at first and then he said-"The whole world wants to know this."

"What?"-He startled-"I didn't understand. 'The whole world wants to know this'; does that mean that nobody has seen him till date?"

His grandpa said with a light smile-"Very few people have seen him. The companies he used to make number one in their field, only their owners knew that how The Business God looks like. Nobody else has seen him."

Tony is seeing his grandpa with dazzling eyes.

His grandpa starts saying again-"Throughout his life, he monopolized 32 companies in their field. Today, the companies which were blessed by God are at no. 1 in their field. He is an amazing personality. When he performs, the corporation industry and entire stock market stage tremble. He has done every illegal work lawfully. CBI, RAW, FBI and all the intelligence agencies around the world are looking for evidence against him. But where does he live? What is his real name and how he looks like? Nobody could find this till date. It seems as if he had removed all the proofs of his existence before living such a life."

"So how did people contact him?"

"People did not contact him; rather he used to contact people. But no police of the world could find about him.

When a company came to number one in its field in a few months, then the whole world understood that The Business God would definitely be behind it, but no one could catch him till today."

He pauses for a while and says again-"The message to The Business God can only be convey by the person whom

The Business God had recently made number one because only that owner knew what the next location of The Business God is."

Tony surprisingly asked-"If police knew this, could not those people still catch The Business God?"

He laughs loudly-"Police...

They could not catch The Business God till date. Every ploy of Business God was done with perfection. And the person who knew how to contact The Business God did not have the courage to tell the police anything.

The head of the entire corporate industry hanged in awe of the name of The Business God.

Business God knew that *half of the combat is won by name only so he had decided that there should be so much terror in his name that before making a conspiracy against him, the terror of his name should force the enemy to bow down.*"

"O My God! I have heard about such a scary character for the first time."- Tony was staring hard at his grandpa.

He smirked in his amazement-"Now, you have been introduced to only one character of this story. There are still more people who would find you more dangerous than him."

"Dangerous than The Business God?"

"Yes, dangerous than The Business God...

His name was Samrat. A stock market king of his time. He was more dangerous than The Business God. Business god used to dominate all the scenarios from behind the curtain but defeating all, Samrat openly challenged that no Government and no police in the world could harm him. Because he had greased everyone's palm. Everything that controls the system, Samrat used to control those things. Print media, digital media, social media, judiciary and even Government also were dance at his tune. What Samrat wanted, only those things and news spread in society. This was reason why the recusancy against him used to be reduced to ashes on its own. There was only one reason behind this and that is 'money'.

He knew this at the age of 15 that *everything is sold in this world; you just have to pay the right price.*

Tony, the sooner you understand this, the better for you that *in this world, the one who has more money, he has more power.*

And the society does not respect those who do not have money, even their own family.

Bitter but this is the reality. Remember that no one will support you in your struggle but when you succeed, the whole world will come to congratulate you."

His grandpa stopped for a while-"Samrat's childhood was passed in an orphanage. In the orphanage, where the parents used to leave their child, who do not have enough money to even arrange for their child's milk.

He named himself Samrat. And he loved to put 'Sikandar' in front of his name because just as Sikandar the great dreamed of conquering the whole world, so did Samrat's dream to rule the whole system.

Samrat lived his childhood in such a way that which take ages for people to understand the things, that orphan Samrat knew those things at the age of 15 to 16 years. Now Samrat had given his full attention in how to play with the mind of these selfish people.

He always believed that *there should be no satisfaction in life because satisfaction is hindrance to up growth* so he has always had a growth mindset. He never liked to join the crowd like ordinary people.

There was a dream in his eyes and passion in the heart that he will become the world's greatest stock market investor. His stock firm will be at number one among all stock firms in the world. His net worth will be bigger than the net worth of all the stock market investor of the world. And with this money, he will rule this world.

Tony, remember one more thing, *we all want success to be achieved as soon as possible but in reality there is no shortcut to success. There is nothing called overnight success, the sooner one wants to jump and reach the higher, sooner he falls into the abyss.*

But Samrat's ideology was different, he believed that to reach a higher destination, one has to jump so high and following this, he chose the wrong path from the beginning.

Every decision taken by Samrat and every single line of his utterance was for the fulfillment of his selfishness. People thought they knew Samrat fully but that was their misunderstanding. People understood the only thing about Samrat that Samrat wanted them to understand. No one could understand Samrat except him till today. He was much cunning than the people of his time. When will he vail and when will he slay, no one can guess this.

He was the only man in the world whose mind was like The Business God, there were some people who were afraid that if Business God and Samrat came together, they will squander the whole world.

Samrat had built a huge empire but he started at the age of 24 with a small detective agency. And after 16 months, a great stock market investor adopted him. He got a built empire. People thought that this was Samrat's fortune, but only Samrat knew what the secret behind it was. Samrat worked 4 years for his Godfather cum father Rudra Pratap Singh. He expanded his empire but 4 years later, his Godfather Rudra Pratap Singh died and half of his

Godfather's legacy now entered the Samrat's name."

"Half legacy?"-Tony asked.

"Yes, half of his legacy.The remaining half of the inheritance was that of Indra, the real son of Rudra Pratap. He had Rudra Pratap's blood but not his intellect. And this thing was very annoying to Indra that his own father does not give him so much respect but trusts that penurious Samrat. Indra was jealous of that Samrat, but he never let this thing be revealed to him. The family that Samrat had got he did not know, whether his family like him or not. But Indra and his step mother Adrika Devi did not love Samrat at all. He felt that Samrat has no right over this wealth rather, the entire right only and only of Indra.

But Samrat was busy expanding that empire. 4 years after the split, the net worth of Samrat was 5 times bigger than that of Indra. In these 4 years, he had built a very strong fort. He takes control many politicians, many news TV anchor, many newspaper editors by giving bribe. He had prepared a large army of YouTubers and bloggers. No bad things could spread in the society against him. But even now there were many people in the system,who were not ready to enslave themselves. But in the view of Samrat, he had the strength and will to buy everyone.

At the time when Samrat started expanding his empire, at that time he joined a way to convert his black money to white money. The police of India did not even know that crores of rupees were being swindled in their very presence. And if they ever knew, those people would not be able to catch Samrat."

"Why?"

"Because that way was completely legitimate. No law could prove him guilty." -his grandpa answered.

"The legal way of converting black money into white

money? Is it even possible?"

His grandpa laughed-*"Nothing is impossible in this world, all you need is courage and to take the right decision at the right time. Then no one can stop you from becoming a prominent figure of the era.*

However, that way of money laundering was round tripping. Where Samrat's money used to reach Mauritius first through Hawala. There is a law in Mauritius that their Government does not disclose the name of the owner of any company.Then there was transfer of that money in the Samrat's Import & Export Company. And then he used that money to buy shares of Indian company through FIIs (Foreign Institutional Investors) by purchasing Participatory Notes (It is an instrument issued by a registered FII to an overseas investor who wishes to invest in Indian stock markets without registering themselves with the market regulator, the Securities and Exchange Board of India). And to show the Government of India, he used to trade that Participatory Notes through endorsement and delivery to himself. And by doing this, he used to convert all his black money into white money."

"O My God! Did the Government know this?"

"Of Course, actually by this way, not only the money of Samrat but the money of many businessmen turned into white. And to be honest this security loops were created by Government itself; because there were many politicians of India who used to convert their black money into white by this way. And this is the reason that neither these holes have been closed in India till now nor will it be closed in future."-his grandpa answered.

"Oh, where the Government itself will be corrupt, it is inevitable to have so much corruption...

By the way, where did his black money came from?"-he asked to his grandpa.

"Yes, I was going to tell that thing...

When Samrat started his detective agency, he needed some smart and reliable people. He has two reliable friends in that orphanage; Ayudh and Udatt. They were also as deserving as they were trustworthy. Samrat had convince them by his satanic plans that they would work for that detective firm during struggle but they would not be named anywhere in any legal documents. So that even if by chance Samrat gets caught by the police so the Ayudh and Udatt can escape unscathed and take forward his mission. Even Ayudh and Udatt had no link between each other.

And when Samrat was adopted by his Godfather i.e. Rudra Pratap Singh then he built two separate large entities by giving money to Ayudh and Udatt from those money got from his Godfather cum father.

The task of Ayudh was to form a very large foundation to by coordinating the NGOs from all over the world. In which great philanthropist and social workers from all over the world will donate money and those money will help people in fields like healthcare and education.

With the help of NGOs, people will get car loans and home loans at cheaper rates than banks but the condition will be that you will have to buy the car what this foundation says and in same way house will also have to be purchased by that real estate firm, from which the foundation will ask to buy. This deal was very much liked by common man as he understood only one thing that he was getting a loan at very low rates but behind all this, the foundation was doing business only through a surpassing marketing strategy through this NGO. Everything was happening according to the corporate law of India, there was nothing illegal. The foundation was named 'Alms-givings' by Ayudh and this foundation was putting down its roots very fast all over the world. But..."

"But what grandpa?"

"This foundation was a medium of whitening Samrat's black money but no one was aware of this. Rather, Ayudh and Samrat were far away from each other in the eyes of the world. Nobody knew this thing that Samrat and Ayudh are childhood friends.

Ayudh carried out illegal work through this foundation in such a way that no one had any doubt about him.

And Ayudh felt that whatever Samrat does, it will be right. Even the whole world understands that there is no link between Samrat and Ayudh, but he will always be Samrat's trusted friend and will never betray him."

"Oh, but how did Ayudh do this, I mean how he converts Samrat's black money into white money?"

"Yes, I am telling you but first listen the story of that trusted friend, Udatt who also supported Samrat in that beautiful journey."

Tony interjected in story-"But a question arising in my mind that when the whole world came to know, Samrat has been adopted by his Godfather Rudra Pratap Singh then didn't the police ever try to find out in which orphanage Samrat grew up?"

His grandpa answered-"Perhaps Samrat had already knew this long ago therefore he had planned this from very beginning. When the three of them left the orphanage, a few days later they stealthily entered the orphanage and burnt all the documents there. There is no information available of any orphaned child not only of those three but for the last 20 years. There those people first burnt their documents and then after that they burnt all the documents there in flames so that they never come under suspicion."

"O my goodness…"

"Yes, I was telling you about Udatt. Like Samrat had given Ayudh the task of put together all the NGOs; in the same way, he gave Udatt the job to unify the real estate agents/brokers around the world. Because he knew that whatever the recession would come in future, the price of the land would always increase so he also invests his money in lands through Udatt's firm.

Samrat and Udatt became friends in the eyes of the world by coming here; because Samrat also used to buy land from the real estate agency of Udatt.

And the same story was Ayudh and Udatt; in the view of world, Ayudh and Udatt came together for the business purpose and they became friends. Whenever 'Alms-givings' foundation buy lands for the purpose of building hospitals or schools, the real estate firm, 'Elevate properties ltd.' donates some money in charity in Ayudh's foundation. Therefore Ayudh's foundation always buys lands through Udatt's real estate firm. Moreover 'Alms-givings' foundation used to force people to buy homes via 'Elevate properties ltd.' through the home loans offered by them. There was running pure business.

And behind all this, they help Samrat to whitening his black money. First, Samrat's black money come in 'Alms-givings' foundation in form of charity through different accounts around the world. And then Ayudh uses that money to buy land via 'Elevate properties ltd.'; which land is already bought by Samrat. So in this way, Samrat's black money turns back to him as return on investment in lands.

Different Swiss accounts that used to transfer money in this foundation belonged to the insiders of Samrat. There is an advantage of opening bank account in Switzerland that the Swiss Government does not share its bank account holder's name and addresses with the any government of the world. But Samrat also knew well that *those in power can never be trusted,* therefore he was constraint to white his black money.

Regardless of how hard the police may search, but they could never prove any link between Samrat and Ayudh; but however Ayudh can get news that how much black money has been donated by Samrat to his foundation recently in the name of charity. And till then Udatt also get the message that again Samrat has decided to convert his black money into white."

"Oh wow, indeed Samrat turned out to be even more dangerous than The Business God, means he was such a sharp minded. He should got the title of Business God."

"You have not yet fully got even with Samrat. Now what I'm telling you, he will become more dangerous in your eyes. I have just given a glimpse of his cunningness. The whole movie is impenitent."

"I am surprised that can a person be even more tremendously freaking talented."

"*Abundant possibilities of development and expansion of intellectual power within each of us exist from our birth itself. A goal is just what is needed and we should divert the flow of all our mental strength towards that goal.*

The only human being who has understood the importance of the intellectual powers abridged within him, has been able to make progress in the world and turning it into an unforgettable talent, he has used all his powers towards a goal.

Samrat knew this therefore he must have had a goal all the time in his life and would try his best to reach his goals at the fastest speed.

As you know Tony, *that person has succeeded whoever has tried something. That person has always failed who spent all his life in wandering his fascinating dreams.*

Samrat, after completing his every goal, set for himself a big goal than his previous one. And he used to make a resolution to himself to walk on the thorn-filled paths. Samrat understood this very well therefore there was no day in his life when he was not focused on his goal because he knows *if there is no goal in life, then his intellectual powers will be devastated in excesses of cupidity, infatuation and lust. And he never wanted to do such foolishness that all his precious energies would be destroyed in such useless deeds."*

Praising Samrat, Tony says-"Really, that was the only thing in Samrat that he had so quickly succumbed to such a huge success in his footsteps.

Okay, tell me more about Samrat...

Let you explain, how he reached this high peak in the stock market."

"When I started telling you about Samrat then I told you that the dream of the Samrat was to become the world's greatest stock market investor. But I also told you that he started with a detective agency. Then it should have to come in your mind that if he wanted to choose the stock market as a career, why did he go to do in the field of espionage...

In fact, by opening a private detective agency, he had misled the world in an illusion trap that his customers are one of the masses. But behind all this, he was making an army of his insiders who used to convey confidential information to Samrat in secret ways. Gradually, his insiders started working as an employee in every big company of India and some insiders had achieved top positions in those companies. And thus he would have already known what is going to happen in the corporate industries like which companies is going to do business deal among themselves, which company is on the brink of being bankruptcy, which products are going to demand in the market etc.

And due to these inside news, the net worth of Samrat was growing day by day.

His insiders used to carry out their activities so intelligently that this thing didn't even get to know the people, where they work like employees. His soldiers used to secretly write secret information on a piece of paper and send it to Samrat. Even before Samrat, that paper used to reach his secretary Mr. Shivraj Datt, the most trusted man of Samrat. Because Samrat knew that the police were keeping a watch on him for 24 hours. Therefore Samrat had entrusted this task to his 55-years-old secretary, Mr. Datt, who was once a loyal secretary of his godfather.

Mr. Datt was a very loyal and deserving person. He had a good grasp of strategy and diplomacy. He worked for Samrat's father Mr. Singh for 15 years; Mr. Singh considered him to be part of his family and he never made his decision without consulting Mr. Datt. As the kings used to have guileless and prudent advisors who never leave their king in any calamity in the same way Mr. Datt was committed to loyalty to Mr. Singh. After the death of Mr. Singh, Mr. Datt chose to be the secretary of Samrat, not of his real son Indra. There was one thing famous among all the stock market firms of Mumbai that Mr. Datt is a very reliable and loyal secretary of Samrat.

There were only two persons among all the stock firms in Mumbai,who knew about such things happening in the future which can either surge in price of stocks of particular company or plunge it. But the whole world praised the talent of picking stocks.

That was a matter of earning profits from stock market, now I wanna tell you something about his black money. It was black money of those 16 stock market investors who used to get to Samrat's Swiss account.

These 16 men started struggle with Rudra Pratap Singh, the Samrat's godfather. And all these people used to invest in the stock market along with their other businesses. These 17 peoples were very close friends among themselves. And these people trusted each other with their eyes closed. All these had become very big businessmen. All these had a good reputation in the society. While sitting in Mumbai, when Samrat used to earn these 16 people a lot of profit with the help of inside news given by his insiders then in return for this, these people put their stolen taxes in Samrat's Swiss account. But this was confined only to Samrat and his father's 16 friends and of course his loyal secretary Mr. Datt.

Because his father also trusted 16 people a lot, that is why Samrat also trusted only these people."

"So, these people were friends of Samrat."

"Hm...Yes, these 16 people and their secretary were friends among themselves...

And also, he had three enemies in this world."

Then Tony asked—"Enemies, and that too three."

"Yes, three enemies.

One of which I have already told you; Samrat's stepbrother Indra. No doubt, Indra had inherited a lot of wealth but how to increase that wealth, he has never learned from his father in all those years. He never respected his father; and not give respect that heritage and why would he do that, he never faced the struggle in life. If he had fought real hard to get that wealth, he would have realized its value.

But at first he could not bear that his father gave the inheritance on which he had full rights, gave it to that con Samrat. He was jealous of Samrat, but at the same time he had realized how clever and black hearted Samrat is. He was just waiting for a chance when he will ruin Samrat completely and force to kneel down in front of him.

He had slight inklings that Samrat was definitely doing some illegal things. Indra presumes that Samrat does not deserve such success so soon. He often used to say that;in the business, only those people can earn the name, who has been seeing since childhood how business is done. He believed that it is necessary to have royal blood to earn the name; otherwise you cannot understand the manoeuvre in businesses. If you are scion of a businessman, only then you can stay remain in business; otherwise, this world does not consider you worthy of that throne. History testifies that after the kings, only their heritor are entitled to their throne, and it is difficult to chimerical this historical convention.

But Indra get enraged every time when he saw increment in Samrat's net worth. He was looking for something that would shake the foundation of Samrat's empire. And now he might have found the one who could even squabble with Samrat."

"Who, The Business God?"

"No, he was the Joint Director of department of investigation of regional office Mumbai of ED (Enforcement Directorate), Aryendra Chauhan, a man who caught many stock market fraudsters red-handed. Many of the young graduates of that time wanted to be like him.

Let me tell you an anecdote of him...

By the way, he has exposed many frauds but the case that I am going to tell you about that case was the first time in his life. It was almost impossible to solve this case with the help of technology of that time. But he solved this case with great emphasis and brought forward the real culprit in front of everyone.

It's 2015; Aryendra was 57 years old at that time, this case was the last case of his life. He had caught the real culprit in his life by getting all his cases to its bottom but he resigned after this case because he knew that there will be many such cases like this in the coming future, but it will be almost impossible to prove the guilt of the culprits. He anyhow solved this case by working day and night but if some more similar cases come up before him, then he will not be able to solve it. Aryendra didn't want to destroy the credibility he had created for so many years. He wanted history to remember him as an officer whose record could not be broken...

That time, when craze of social media was taking effect on people of India. When social media platforms were expanding very fast, many such hackers were also emerging who wanted to antagonize those social media sites. There were many hackers who had the skills to hack the social media accounts. These hackers get caught after so many efforts.

And one person took advantage of it...

There was a company among some famous automobile companies of that time, 'Force Motors Ltd.'. This company is India's largest van maker. It ranks 327th (2016) amongst India's fortune 500 companies list. Aside from manufacturing light transport vehicles, it also makes engines and axles, as well as a large variety of die-cast aluminum parts. At that time the share price of this company was around Rs. 3000. And the performance and graph of the company was growing up every year. But perhaps there was something that causes a big jump in the share price of this company.

June 14, 2015;

In the board meeting, the chairman of the company 'Force Motors Ltd.', Abhay Firodia says-"Our Company is going to create a history. Today is a great pleasure for a company that our company is awarded a contract by BMW, resulting which we will produce and test engines for all BMW Cars and SUVs of India. We are going to inaugurate a new plant in Chennai which will be able to produce up to 20,000 engines per year.

That force facility will assemble four- and six-cylinder engines for seven BMW models- the 1-series, 3-series, 5-series, 7-series, X1, X3 and X5 here."

That board meeting room resounds with thunderous applause.

Then the managing Director of the company, Prasan A. Firodia says-"You guys already knew about this contract. And in a few days, we will give notice of this to SEBI (Securities and Exchange Board of India). By the way, today, you all have been called to tell you the date of that inauguration."

"Yes and the date is July 21, 2015. We have deliberately set this date on Thursday. Because this is such big good news for our company and for our shareholders, therefore after the release of this news on Thursday, the share price of our company will increase significantly on Friday. And then when the market will closed for two days after that; on Monday, there will be higher chances of increasing the price of our company's stock"-Abhay said.

Everyone is applauding his idea.

Sitting Abhay says again-"So with whose auspicious hands, inauguration should be done?"

All are looking at each other with smiling and radiant face and thinking about this.

Then, an Executive Director, Veda Mishra says-"In my view, union cabinet minister for heavy industries and public sector/enterprises, Anant Geete should be invited for this."

"You are right"-the chairman made a nod on this-"And also we have to call the state minister for industries and steel of the Tamil Nadu, Thiru Thangamani."

All the people agreed.

June 21, 2015;

It is 09:00 AM, Veda is preparing for go to a hill station. And keeping his personal laptop in bags, he says to some employees of his office, who came to his home for helping Executive Director of their company-"You guys don't stop me now, I'll be back in 6-7 days."

Employees have to give in to their boss's insistence.

Then Veda moves his hand towards the cell phone which is placed on his dining table, but accidentally a jug filled with water spilled on his phone and water entered in his phone. Now a problem arises that when Veda will enjoy in hill station, how will he contact with the people of his company.

Then an employee of his company, Prabhas says to Veda-"Don't worry sir, give me that mobile, I'll make repair this.

It seems that God also wants you to spend time with your family in pleasure."

Now it is decided that Veda will enjoy with his family at the hill station without any tension.

June 22, 2015;

The stock price of 'Force Motors Ltd.' closed at Rs. 2,996.22 on previous day but opened today at Rs. 2,959.00.

Prabhas calls his office at 09:00 AM and says that he is going to Australia for his routine checkup; and Prabhas took 5 days off.

At that day 12 o' clock, a tweet comes on Veda's twitter account, in which it is written;

I want to apologize to all our company's shareholders; I want to tell all of you that I have sold all my shares because after 2-3 days you will know about the scams of our company. And I know that our company will be bankrupt therefore I am requesting all of you to sell your shares soon otherwise all your money will be squandered and you guys will be plundered.

After this post, there is a hectic rush in the stock market and all the stock holders are selling the shares of 'Force Motors Ltd.' and the company which can be multibagger in future was becoming a multibegger. It was coming in everyone's mind that when an Executive Director of the company is saying this from his twitter account, then it will be definitely true.

Today, already there was gap down opening for the company, and it had reached Rs. 3,033.62 before 12:00 but after this tweet, downfall is starting. Price is going down.

The company's CEO, Managing Director and all the employees are worrying that why Veda did this. Everyone knew that he had done it against the law, so now he may have to go to jail. But no one is able to contact him.

When Veda opened the laptop to see his company's stock growth at the hill station, he saw that the stock value of his company is decreasing. And when the stock price stopped going down from Rs. 2,918.00, he bought shares of his company in huge amount and with an investment of Rs.

8.5 Crores; he bought 2.3% stakes of his company. Because Veda knew that when after a few days, we announce that contract deal with BMW in public, then the value of the stock will definitely increase and also his gain on his capital will be increase. But perhaps he did not know there is an atmosphere of fear among the people in the stock market at this time.

Here, the CEO of the company Abhay Firodia lodged an FIR on Veda that he tried to ruin the credibility of the company.

After 5 days, when Veda returned from flight after enjoying his vacation then coming down the flight stairs, he saw that on one side, there are some employees of his company and next to them is Joint Director of ED, Aryendra Chauhan and some policemen with him.

Aryendra goes ahead and handcuffs Veda. Veda and his family all go flabbergasted to see what he has done because of which police are arresting Veda.

But later when Aryendra inquires with Veda and his employees, it is revealed that Veda did not even have his phone, his phone went defective due to water infused in it; Prabhas took his phone for getting it repaired. First, the cyber cell took Veda's laptop and Aryendra started searching for Prabhas but he came to know that he is on leave from many days. And he went to Australia for his routine checkup.

On the second day, Aryendra and Veda described the whole truth by convening a press conference and Veda acquitted of all charges with honour. And the whole charge hit Prabhas.

When the whole truth is known to the people, then the atmosphere of terror is slightly reduced.

After 2 days, Veda receives Aryendra's call-"When

your employee Prabhas getting off the plane and coming towards the office, we arrested him."

The company's Executive Director and some of his special employees arrive at the regional office of ED in Mumbai then they came to know that Prabhas is being interrogated.

After half an hour, Prabhas came in front of everyone and says-"I am not guilty. I did not do anything wrong. I immediately went and gave your phone to the service center and the receipt which I got from that service center; I gave it to the police. I am inculpable.

And I was coming a few days ago but where I used to go for my routine checkup, the hospital where I usually go, there was a strike of doctors. Therefore I was able to come today. As soon as I got off the flight, I was coming to the office so that I finish my work first, then I will go home and rest. But the police arrested me on the way that too in the crime that I tweeted from your twitter account to downgrade the image of our company."

Interrupting the conversation, Aryendra says-"Mr. Veda, the man who was repairing your phone, he has not been on the job at the service center since the second day. We suspect that he hacked your twitter account by stealing data from your mobile and tweeted on June 22.

So now, you can take Prabhas back. Soon I will bring the real culprit in front of you.

Have a nice day, everyone."

Then Aryendra goes a little far and starts doing some work and here the police are stand around Veda, Prabhas and all those employees. Till now Veda was just looking at Prabhas; then he says-"Prabhas, you must be tired. Go home and relax and come from tomorrow."

Prabhas interjaculated-"Sir, I am innocent but still, in

the eyes of you guys, if I have done something wrong, then forgive me."

Veda puts both his hands on Prabhas's shoulders-"Prabhas, always remember one thing in life, *you need to apologize only if you are sure that you made a mistake. There is no need to apologize for what people think about you.*

And anyway, Mr. Chauhan has also said that he will bring the real culprit in front of us. So, don't be worry, go home and relax."

Everyone was listening to these things, and everyone feels that Prabhas is not guilty.

July 21, 2015;

The engine plant was inaugurated by union cabinet minister for heavy industries and public sector/enterprises Anant Geete, In the presence of Thiru Thangamani, the Tamil Nadu state minister for industries, steel, mines and minerals as already planned. After announcement, share price is surging as expectedly. This share is attracting a large no. of intraday traders.

On July 22, this share opens at Rs. 3,000.23 and reached its peak at Rs. 3,245.54 and gave 8.18% return to its shareholders in intraday trading.

Gradually, its share price is increasing day by day. On August 01, it reaches its maximum at Rs. 3,449.76; shareholders are very optimistic.

Two months passed, Veda had also bought its 2.3% stakes so he has also made great progress in his life.

But here, Mr. Chauhan's colleagues were beginning to doubt his ability because this was probably the first such case in his life that took Aryendra more than one month to solve. But till now the real culprit not fell into the clutches of Aryendra. But still Aryendra was investigating the evidence and witnesses by working day and night.

And one day, when Veda was reading newspaper, sitting in his yard.A car stopped in his gate;and Aryendra comes towards him with some of his officers. Veda welcomes them all and brings them inside his bungalow which he had registered 20 days ago in his own name. Veda asked-"So guys, what bring you here? Was the real culprit caught?"

Aryendra answered with a smile-"Not yet, but after one an hour he will be behind the bars."

Expressing wonder, Veda says-"Oh... so, you know that who is the guilty."

"Before one month, when I was tired of looking for the man who repaired your mobile in the service center, when I was tired of this case, I started to investigate this case from another point of view and I interrogated all the witnesses again.

Then I get to know one thing; you employees were saying that very few water was infused in your mobile but the owner of service center was saying that it seemed as if someone had kept your mobile immersed in water for 10 minutes.

At that time, I suspected two people. One was your loyal employee Prabhas and the second one was you.

So, I suspected you that maybe there was not enough water in the mobile to damage your mobile. But you intentionally sent to repair that mobile and you have already told someone the login ID and password of your twitter account and assigned him to tweet that thing in the fixed time. And when holidaying at the hill station, you would have seen that your company's stock price is decreasing. You would have guessed that your man has done the work that you had entrusted him. And quickly you invested Rs. 8.5 Crores in your own company and took ownership of 2.3% of the company. Because you knew very well that a very big deal of your company is going to be announced in public in a few weeks and after that the share price of your company would go increase with which you would book a lot of profit as it actually happened.

He began laughing-"Good story, but you cannot arrest me on the basis of the plea of more or less water infused on the phone. If you have any strong evidence against me, then talk about putting me behind bars."

"First, listen to me carefully Mr. Veda". There was dominating influence in his voice.

"Yes yes, of course, actually you should have become a story teller. How you struck in this profession?"

"Okay... let you tell me, when you gave your mobile to Prabhas, what was the exactly time?"

"I might have given him that mobile about 11:00 AM in the morning."

"You are right, but let me tell you one thing that he gave your mobile to the service center at 01:16 PM; however the distance between your home and service center will take hardly 20 minutes. In these two hours neither was he in his home nor did he go to office. When we started investigating this thing closely, we came to know that Prabhas's mobile and the location of your mobile were showing on the same day from 11:45 AM to 12:30 PM in the parking lot of a hotel in this city. Then when we went to see that CCTV footage of that parking lot, we came to know that all the cameras in the parking lot went bad two days ago. Your employee Prabhas had a good luck. Then he must have put that mobile in water for about 10 minutes. I started to doubt him more on this matter. We started investigating why Prabhas left for Australia the next day. And again there is a coincidence, all the doctors of the hospitals in which he used to get his routine checkup were on strike, due to which he was delayed in coming back to India. What a great drama was hatched by your employee Prabhas."

Veda smirked in his plea-"But you also cannot arrest Prabhas. Can't he go to that parking lot? It is also possible that he has gone there for some of his personal work. There is no enough power in your story, Mr. Aryendra..."

Aryendra suddenly stands up and orders his officers-"Arrest him."

"What? But why? Why are you arresting me?

When you are saying that Prabhas has done this, why am I being handcuffed?"

Smiling he comes near to Veda-"Listen Mr. Veda, I know very well that you are the real culprit. You are the mastermind of this show and Prabhas, at your behest, first make defected all the cameras in the parking lot and then he gave all the secret data to the hacker. At your behest, he left for Australia next day in the morning and according to plan, hacker hacked your twitter account and tweeted that thing which caused to shove to your company's share price. And when you monitored the stock price at that hill station, so you understand that hacker has done his job. And you got shares of your company in dirt cheap rate.

So, am I right, Mr. Veda?"

Laughing on these things, Veda's face suddenly changes into a sardonic pose-"You have such a good presuming power but proving this in court, your entire system will be sweated out."

He laughed out loud-"Never in my entire life I ever given such an opportunity to someone that charge of my case have been given to anyone. No one has broken my record till date and how did you even think that without solving this case completely, I would ever show you my face."

He gibes at his utterance-"Stop wasting your time...

You also very well know that you have no such strong evidence against me which can effrontery to put me behind the bars."

Aryendra lays his eyes on him and snaps his fingers.

Then his one of his officers enters with a man who is already handcuffed. He takes him stand in front of Veda.

Taking a deep breath in rage, he lowers his eyes by this checkmate. It seems his game is over now.

But a proud smile comes over Aryendra's unblinking face-"Look on that person, he is your childhood friend, isn't he? Who is now a doctor in Australia and what a coincidence he is doctor in that hospital where Prabhas used to go for his routine checkup and another interesting part of the story, he is that person who started the strike in that hospital.

So, am I right?... Mr. mastermind...

You have made such a good plan but you made a mistake...

Wanna listen due to which you are going to jail?"

Veda is staring at him, then Aryendra says-"Okay, let me tell you...

That blunder was to tell the whole plan to this doctor. You know, what he did then.

There was a deal between you and him that he would arrange that strike and you will give him $100,000 for that but thirst of money increased in his mind and first he short huge amount of shares of your company then he invested in your company by that money which is given by you as advance. And because of this, he caught. And if you want more evidence, then the call records is enough.

Aryendra clapped his hands in cunningness of Veda-"You used your brain very slyly. Such a scam that no one could doubt you and you also acted amazingly. A scammer like you, has rarely came into contact with me whom I praised. Would that you hadn't made the mistake of trusting this doctor, you would have been independent today. Being such a big businessman, how did you make the mistake of trusting someone completely? *One should trust either on God or on oneself.* But you will now be able to reap the benefit of this edification only in the next birth."

Lowering his voice, Veda says-"Let's make a deal; in which I will benefit but you will get profit more."

Aryendra laughed-"I like very much this flair of the businessmen that you guys understand that a businessman can buy anyone in this world but candidly saying, I don't want any speckle on my credibility."

"What nonsenses, was it not a blot on your credibility to not catch Samrat Singh 'Sikandar'?"

Aryendra gave him a smack across the face and commands officers to take them away and lock them in the same prison where Prabhas is kept as a captive.

Tony says-"Grandpa, I am convinced of Aryendra's intellect how he used to arrest criminals by putting his mind to it.

But why did he slap Veda, when he said about Samrat?"

If you touch anyone on the raw, he will definitely scream. The wise one here is the one who caress the raw nerve and make believe the front person that he is a true well-wisher of him and after it he make use of him for the benefit of himself. Because if you help someone in their misery, then that person will be considered as the Angel sent by God and then he will be ready to sacrifice his life for you.

But here, Veda did just opposite.

Aryendra started his career journey with much struggle and then he revealed many stock market scams in no time and gradually he went on to become a super cop.

Most of the fraudsters, he used to catch in the scams were enemies of Samrat, many of them even gave Samrat an open challenge. When Aryendra caught them and interrogate them, each time he got some clues which tells that Samrat has also done many frauds but Aryendra and his team could never find out about that frauds. Those people never got single evidence against Samrat. It was also known to the teammates of Aryendra and his officers that he wants to expose Samrat by hook or by crook. But no one knew this thing outside his office because Aryendra had forbidden everyone not to leak this thing out. Because he believed that *the enemy should never know that you are very hostile to him.*

He was about 48 years old at that time,he was a true patriot in the eyes of Aryendra's teammates and the people of India. But there was one thing that vex his teammates a lot that Aryendra never told his teammates, who his secret agents are? Every time he refused to give their information because these were the agents with whose help he could get a high position in his department. And he absolutely did not want anyone else can become his competitor by using his agents. He had achieved that position by lots of maneuvering and he did not want anyone else to be eligible for that position while he is in service."

"Wow, what a character.

But let you tell me first, who is the real hero of this

story?

Samrat Singh 'Sikandar' or 'The Business God'?"

"Hero is the one who has a character, a good character; who along with his progress has done well for the people. Who fight to get his right not try to usurp anyone's right; who faces many difficulties, but never gives up; one who does not lose patience even in the most difficult situation. And he used to put his mind in the well-being of the people, that one is the real hero. The real hero is never scared out because he knows that he is on the right track. He never fazed, even if the whole world turns against him. But he knows that he is on the right path so he never has the fear of death and he utterly destroyed all the evil people by eradicating them. This is what a true hero is."

"Really, how proud is it to be a hero..."

"No one is inborn hero; the hero is made by fighting the whole world on his own. He succeeds on his own and becomes a hero. And in reality, that view is worth seeing when everyone wants to bang you on the ground but you fight with them and rule them by reaching first on the top. And you tell the whole world that there is no one in this world better than you. It takes a lot of struggle to become a true hero in this world."

"Of course."

"And who is the hero of this story, you will find out by yourself at the end of the story.

Okay?"

"Okay, grandpa."

"Now, I am going to tell you one more character of this story...

That one is also a stock market investor and of course a royal blood, Gajendra Rai, the owner of 'Rai Securities Ltd.'. A very trusted man in the field of stock market, and of course his stock firm is the most trusted firm of India.

You can say, he was a big bull of stock market of his time, and he had learned all the tricks to take over the entire stock market investor from his father who was also a great stock investor of his time.

Gajendra was also the owner of 'RFAM Group' which was leading company in insurance and asset management services.

He made lots of millionaire through the stock market, so they also used to enounce his brand name. In the gathering where he used to go, everyone's head bowed down on their own.

And just like it, Samrat wants the monopoly in stock market."

"Monopoly, that too in the field of stock market?"

"Sounds odd, isn't it? That a company anyhow can achieve monopoly by makings its product/service exceptionally valuable but in the field of stock market, no one can make 100% prediction of which company's stock price will increase or decrease the next day. Then how can anyone achieve monopoly in this field.

But Samrat dreamed it and this was his perversity that one day he will be the king of the entire stock market and *history is a witness that the entire universe give in to the insistence of humans.* And it happened...

Samrat knows, only one man can satisfy his insistence, Gajendra Rai. But how, he was just looking for that opportunity which can fulfill his dream.

THREE

"There is no curse in this world ahead of indigence. A poor person is get to pocketing insults from his kinsfolk, friends and from even his family and it is not over, but he also has to be insulted by his wife every day. In today's world, every person being exploits the poor and by taking advantage of their compulsions, they continue to make them poorer."

- Samrat Singh 'Sikandar'

And one day in Gajendra's stock firm;

Gajendra exits his cabin, drawing everyone's attention he says-"Today, I have decided to award 'Broker of the year' to any one of you."

Everyone is getting excited; who is that lucky guy who will get this award this year? This year, there are only three guys who are deserving of this award –Kavish, Mahidhar and Sujal. Sujal was working for last 2 years; Kavish and Mahidhar were working for the last 3 years. This year, these three have earned the highest return to this firm.

"Any guess..."

Many names are echoing from that crowd.

Then he announce-"So, "Broker of the year' awards goes to...

Kavish...who has earned highest profit for this firm,

this year.

And I announce that from today onwards he will be a senior broker of this firm."

Gajendra quietly says in his ear-"Come to my cabin after 10 minutes".

After some time when Kavish is in his boss's office; his boss says-"You would know that there was a loyal and honest employee, Durjay who was also my personal advisor. I trusted him very much but he turned out to be an insider and now I am entrusting you for those works. From today you will have an important role in the growth of this firm. Can I trust you completely?"

"100% sir, you can trust me blindly. I will never break up your trust. And I will work day and night for the growth of this firm. I'll wreck all the enemies. Now you can be unworried about my concern."

"Good.

Now you can go"

After he leaves, Gajendra says to his secretary Salila-"Tail our detectives behind him. I have seen that traitor Durjay's treachery. Now there is no one should be trusted."

Next day;

By the way, the owners of many stock firms used to come to meet Gajendra Rai, but on that day all the brokers of 'Rai Securities Limited' were surprised, when they saw that Samrat came today. Samrat enters Gajendra's cabin with his secretary Mr. Datt.

Mr. Datt says to secretary of Gajendra, Salila-"Today is our appointment."

She says-"Yes, and boss is waiting for you."

Gajendra cast of mind that today this person's ego has crumbled. Today, another owner of a stock firm will kneel down in my footsteps.

He welcomes him and asks him to sit and then says to his secretary, Datt-"Welcome Datt, loyalists like you are rarely seen."

And then he says to Samrat-"Samrat, I know your father well, the glare of his name spread with great fanfare. He did nothing wrong by adopting you.

So, what brings you here?"

Samrat says-"Mr. Rai, now I know that it is good to be with everyone in this field. And I'm sure that you will not turn down the initiative of our friendship."

He holds out his hand towards Rai;staring him, Gajendra thinks that everyone comes here to sycophancy and he has come to befriend me. But after some time, being deep in thought, he shakes hands with him and says-"Let's make a new story of friendship"

"Of course.

Let's initiate with it from a joint venture..."

I'm proposing joint venture insurance named 'Rudra Insurance Management Arm (RIMA)' which offers general insurance including motor insurance, health insurance, travel insurance and home insurance to across the world and that too in leastways legal formalities which will our USP (Unique selling proposition).

My brokerage firm, 'Singh Broking Solutions'is the leading brokerage firm having 13.64% market share and your assets management firm is the biggest firm of India; and when we come together, no one can compete us."

Then Mr. Datt gives a file to his secretary; he says again-"It has all the details of that joint venture. You will be able to take a decision easily."

"Okay, I'll think about it"-Gajendra said with a grin.

"So, to celebrate this friendship, I am organizing a party after a few days, you have to come."

"Yeah sure, I'll come."

Standing up, Samrat says-"So, done. Let's meet at the party."

After he leaves, Gajendra asks his secretary to send for Kavish. When Kavish is sitting in front of him, he says-"Kavish, you must have seen that Samrat came here; he proposed friendship and offers to work together in a joint venture insurance.

What you think, we should accept this deal or not?"

Thinking for a while, he says-"Politics says that we should always support the dominant people and today 'Singh Broking Solutions' is in the dominant position in the market; they gave maximum return to its customers, especially to its swing investors/ short term investors and the mindset of the people has always been that they wanna get rich as soon as possible, taking advantage of this thinking, this firm has reached so high so soon. We will also benefit greatly if our assets management company take part with it."

"But what will he gain from this deal?"

"They will get more customers easily and by the way sir, you are now a big brand that's why he approaches you and didn't go anywhere else.

But sir, however, he is a businessman; in any deal, he will first calculate his own profit then that of the person in front."

"You are absolutely right here."

"Why not we do an experiment with this deal; after a year, we will know whether this deal will be beneficial for us or not?"

"Your words have some merit.

Let's do that."

After 8 days;

Gajendra asks his secretary that what she gets knew when she assigned the detective behind him. Then she tells that their detective has all information about him. He has only his parents in his house and he is not married yet. He has a simple 2 BHK flat; and we have checked all information about him like his bank accounts, call details etc.; and he is not selling our information outside anywhere else.

He gets amused at this thing-"Good... tell Kavish that tomorrow Samrat is organizing a party at his bungalow, and he has to come with me in that party and also you too."

Next day;

It is 11:30 PM, everyone has gone after enjoying the party from Samrat's bungalow; there are only a few special guests, staying at home. In main hall, there is Samrat's wife Nivedita Arya, Rai's secretary Salila and his employee Kavish and Mr. Datt.

In upper hall; chalice of wine in their hands and Samrat calls his servant for send his wife in that room. After some time, his wife reached in that room with a gift in her hands and moves towards Gajendra.

Samrat utters-"This is our first keepsake of our friendship. We would be glad if you accept it."

"Okay, but what is in it?"

When he takes off the wrappings; suddenly Samrat says-"This watch is worth of Rs. 80,000. The built figures and designs in this are crafted with world's most expensive diamonds. The hands of this watch and almost 75% of the machinery are made of platinum. The chain of this watch is alloy of gold and platinum and the glass is the world's costliest glass which is made in Belgium."

"But I can't accept such a costliest present, please."

"Oh c'mon, it is nothing in front of your personality, don't deny; this special is made for you only."

After much refusal, he finally accepts that watch.

After some time, Gajendra says to Samrat-"Enough about businesses, now let's talk something else."

Samrat smiles-"Okay, as you wish."

After taking a sup of wine, Gajendra says-"I read an interview of you in a business magazine, in which you have said that you wanted to become a businessman since childhood. So, when your childhood was spent in an orphanage where you could not even understand the 'b' of business, then why aspire to become a businessman?"

Samrat smirked and took a sip, without blinking his eyes he started staring the floor. Rai was waiting for his answer and after a while, he says-"Whoever left me in that orphanage to live without the shade of parents, he was my father or my mother, I don't know but know that they didn't have enough money to feed me to keep me alive. Getting young, when I got to know this thing since then I always bear in mind that *a person cannot be happy without money. Money is very very important for pleasure and peace in life.*

A penniless person, while alive, is like a spiritless person. If he is penurious, then his life has no meaning because he has no power to give effect to any role.

The orphanage I grew up in was a shanty town; I have observed those people very closely, I have read the mindset of all kinds of people and tried to learn about humans.

There I learned that *there is no curse in this world ahead of indigence. A poor person is get to pocketing insults from his kinsfolk, friends and from even his family and it is not over, but he also has to be insulted by his wife every day. In today's world, every person being exploits the poor and by taking advantage of their compulsions, they continue to make them poorer.*

I didn't want to live such a life; I don't like to look back at those periods of my life. Yes, I do help the poor, but I was so done with that life, the memory of that shameful life still haunts me at every turn. At every moment, I remind myself of my past, and keep fretting that I don't want to see such days back and those horrifying scenes keep inspiring me that I have to become more wealthy and to earn more money so that I can help more people."

He stands up and says again-"So, I have decided that by becoming the richest person, I'll show myself to the selfish world full of boisterousness. They rob the poor and I'll rob them. There will be so much money, I have; that no one has the courage to incur my hostility. I have complete financial freedom; the things that will my eyes to rest on for a while, that thing will be only mine. I'll not need to think about money to buy anything in the world." His tone was calm but filled with confidence.

He moves toward Rai and looking him in the eye-"One day, I will be the richest person of the universe whom the world will worship."

Gajendra only gazing at him in astonishment and he swigged the wine in a gulp. And close to Samrat, shaking hand he says-"I'm very glad to befriend personality like you."

"But I am happy even more than you that today the king of the stock market has become my friend."

He urges him to sit again, and then Rai asks-"Well, have you never been afraid that what happens if you end in smoke?"

He looks at Rai with a twinkle in his eye-"Fear of failure?...

My thinking is slightly different from the rest of the people, perhaps that's why I have been able to reach the top so soon.

I believe that...

The fear of failure gives you the victory. Those who take this fear seriously, their goal at every step gages their preparedness; all the time the goal will frighten us that there should be no minor mistake in the preparations. Who drawing a blank by this fear and who depends on their destiny, they do not know due to this fear, perfection can come in their work. The more seriously one takes this fear, the greater the chance of victory bowing in his footstep."

"All I can praise you, is less.

Okay, what is the success, according to you?"

"There should be positive thinking, even your plan sounds fancy, you should believe in it and you should leave laziness to make it successful.

Those who build the great empire, they had dreamed it first and with complete dedication, they have transformed that dream into reality. There should be only will power; first wish for anything and then desire it strongly and be prepared for any kind of sacrifice to turn it into reality, and then victory will be yours."

"So, what is your strategy for those troublesome

enemies while walking on these paths?"

He take a pause, while pouring out the wine in chalices of both, he says-"*If we leave behind the enemies who are causing hardship us, then one day they will all join together and they will stab the daggers in our back. So, according to me, people who cause trouble have no right to live. They should be exterminated a put an end to their entire existence. If you want to achieve the dreams and become deserving to get the destination, you have to become a murderer of the difficulties of the way.*"

He looks at Rai-"*The only cure of thorns of the way is to keep their nose quashed with shoes.*"

Rai is thinking that today he met with the ever enigmatically dangerous person.

Both are looking at each other in the eyes, and they smiled.

FOUR

In this world, first of all, people destroy the one who is the most direct, innocent and good, but no one dares to wrangled with evil person just like that the first straight trunk trees are cut in the forest but no one touches the warped and knotty trees.

It's 05:00 AM in the morning; and Samrat is in his dream. In that dream, he sees his past happening in front of his eyes. This was the dreadful time that Samrat has been hated the most and even today, those days keep haunting him in the dream that he might not have to live that life again.

Samrat spent 18 years of his life in that orphanage which is situated in Dharavi, Bombay; but one day he tried to become an independent bird. The 12 years old Samrat, wearing a sloppy white half-shirt and half pant, leaps over the orphanage wall at 02:00 AM in the night with a water bottle in his hand. Now he is a free bird; nobody is going to put restrictions on him. Now he can do anything, whatever he wants.

It is morning; strolling, he sat to the next to the gate of the wall of a bank. There is rush of vehicles and rickshaws in the road; and many people are getting in and out in the bank. But there is no security guard at the gate. There are many shops on the other side of the road- grocery store, stationary, confectionary, barber's saloon and many more.

He feels thirsty, no more water in his bottle, and after some time he is feeling very hungry along with thirst and the scorching sun is on his head. Sometimes he is looking up at the sky and sometimes at the grocery store in front. Some people are talking next to that grocery store.

Just then the security guard came out from inside the bank and told Samrat to flee from there, reprimanding him. What could he do; he went to the other side of the road and sat down on the ground next to the saloon; and started observing those guys and the bank which is in front of him now. He sees two men come out of the bank, in a perfectly formal dress and both go in different directions, and both had a silver color suitcase in their hands. At that time, he hears the voice from those guys, 'Cocaine'. Samrat well knew what it is, an addictive drug which smuggling is illegal; and who help to get these people caught, they get a lot of money in reward. He heard some more things that if you want cocaine, then meet me after an hour at back at the St. Anthony's Church. But Samrat thought that what does he have to do with it, he doesn't want to be in that fuss.

Just then there is hue and cry inside the bank, which clamour is heard outside, that guard closes then gate of the bank, and shortly thereafter several police jeeps arrive there.

Then entering the saloon, a man says-"A theft has been occurred in the bank; people there are saying that maybe the thief was wearing a black color suit and he had a silver color bag in his hand.

And who will help to get those people to catch, he will get Rs. 10,000 reward from the police."

When Samrat hears this, he thinks that the guard, seeing my sloppy clothes and my condition, had considered me a thief, but the real thief had came in very well dress.

Samrat now understood very well that how much do your clothes matter. *If your clothes are neat and clean then you'll get respect and if clothes are sloppy and dirty then you'll be considered a thief. No person tries to understand the personality of the person in front, one is worshiped and get respect because only of his outer appearance.* He now understood that *however a person is internally, but if he has money and expensive clothes then in the eyes of the world, he is considered a respectable person.*

He is now feeling ravenously hungry; and repeatedly in his mind, the last line spoken by that man is echoing that the one will be get rewarded who helps to catch that thief.

He cast of mind that he doesn't know where the thief is now but he knows where the smuggling of cocaine will be done. So, he thinks that if he wants to earn money through rights ways, he has to get those people caught who are on wrong paths. Only by catching those cocaine smugglers can he get some money in reward with which he can satisfy his hunger pangs. He now decided to get them caught and moves towards the Dharavi police station.

When he reached the police station, he saw a police officer sitting outside on his bike and reading a newspaper. Samrat moves toward him and tells him that he can get the smugglers involved in cocaine smuggling. Staring him, the police officer says–"Do you know, who smuggles cocaine and where does its smuggling happen?"

"I don't know who they are but know that after some time they will smuggle the cocaine at back of the church."

After staring at him for a while, he looks towards the police station and then says to him–"Sit back on the bike with me."

Sitting on the bike Samrat says–"Won't we go in a jeep?"

After he doesn't answer, Samrat again asks after a while-"Why didn't you call more policemen with you?"

But that officer kept riding the bike quietly, after some time he asks one more question-"How much money will I get due to help to catch those people? I'm hungry since morning and I've not eaten anything. But I thought that I would not make money through evading or any other wrong way and I'll satisfy my hunger by earning money from right path."

But again seeing him silent, he becomes a bit disappointed. They reached the church, and parking his bike next to the main gate, he asked him to get off the bike.

Now that police officer grasps the hand of him vigorously and dragged in him to the back of the church. When both of them reached behind the church, they saw three men standing there. On seeing the police, one of them runs away snatching a packet from the hand of one, both smugglers are not afraid to see the police and remain stand there. They both first see the police and then the 4 feet boy; that is when the police officer drags in Samrat in front of them and tells-"You don't know ever how to do business properly and dreamed to become a drug mafia."

"What happened due to which you came here to teach us to how to do business?"

"If this boy had approached to any other police officer except me, then you guys would have been behind the bars at this time.

He knew everything about you, fools; even exact time and place."

Both of them are angrily glowering at Samrat, they tell him to not get panic, and they promised they will handle him.

That police officer again says-"Be careful. If he comes

again to the police station, I'll not be able to help you, guys.

And yes, I'll charge extra commission for this."

Samrat is trembling with fear and he forgets about his hunger and thirst now by this fear but one thing he is repeating in his mind that the one who supports the truth wins only.

After that officer leaves, both men surround Samrat. And they started beating him, and then they turned him on the ground; and started spurning him.

Samrat repeatedly shouts, saying "please, don't thwack on me...

I was just hungry, so I thought that I'll get some money when I get you catch...

Leave me, please. I'll not tell anyone anything."

But those people are not hearing anything and along with kicking him, they are threatening him that after today he should not be seen even around the police station, otherwise they will do worse than this with him. He is half-dead now; then those men together hold the hands and feet of him and throws that half-dead Samrat in the gutter next to them.

Then Samrat gets up from the bed in fear, his face is covered in sweat and a kind of awe is reflected in his face, that dreadful scene is still in before his eyes. When he looks around, he finds that he was sleeping on his bed with his wife and what he has seen so far was his past which came as a nightmare.

He gets up from the bed and stands in front of the mirror placed at some distance; and starts looking himself in the mirror. Without blinking his eyes he is thinking, *there is no benefit in showing goodness by staying in the midst of sinful people.*

If you try to satisfy your stomach with the right paths, then evil people come and ruin you and throw you in the gutter. In this world, first of all, people destroy the one who is the most direct, innocent and good, but no one dares to wrangled with evil person just like that the first straight trunk trees are cut in the forest but no one touches the warped and knotty trees.

This world is full of selfish and depraved people that they do not care about hunger or thirst of anyone else. All of them are trying to fill their paunch by ruining others.

If you want to live properly in this world, then you have to rule on these selfish people; we have to keep them all under our power and vigor or else this world will not let us live.

Now Samrat calls Mr. Datt and asks to him-"How many details of people you get, this month?"

"Sir, 25."

"Okay, send them money order of Rs. 2,500 from my Swiss bank account.

And it should be done in a week."

Then disconnecting the phone, he prepares to go to the office.

Tony asks to his grandpa-"To whom did Samrat send the money?"

"He used to help those who were not capable to earn money; the aim of his life was to take care of helpless children, senile human being, and mentally sick person. That was the driving force due to which he became such wealthy person.

Would that world knows this secret; no one knows this except Samrat and his secretary that a kind man is hidden inside a sly businessman, even his wife doesn't know about this."

"But why, why he didn't do publicity of this great work.

Today's social workers and philanthropists shout on social media that how they helped poor, but he didn't tell this even to his wife, why?"

"He used to take his any action very cautiously; he was not one to draw public attention from the publicity of his good work.

First, this kindness was his weakness and he kept his weakness hidden from all; and second, if the people had known this, then he would have to give details about his Swiss account due to which the secret of his black money get revealed and he could be arrested. All these were the reason why he didn't make it public.

Samrat was a genius stock market investor even though for the world but internally he was a Robin Hood robbing the rich and help the people. From inside, he was a kind man who used to help those who were truly helpless.

But no one could get a sense of this weakness; therefore he had decorated his worldly life with expensive items. Sometimes, he used to spend extravagantly, which he didn't like, but to show this world that Samrat has no pity on the poor, he also had to do this useless expenditure.

As I already told you that Samrat used to do exactly the same things so that the world would exactly think of what he wanted; and in reality, no one would able to know what kind of person Samrat is?

Dwelling in the biggest slum of Asia, Samrat had felt poverty very closely and of course the affliction of the rich.

This was the reason, that circumstances forced him to become such a man that he would rob the rich and help the poor."

"From your utterance, it seems that the real hero of this story is Samrat, isn't he?"

"Even though, his motive may be good but the path he chose was wrong and a person who is in wrong path can never be a hero.

Okay...

Let me continue the story...

After 25 days;

Samrat is sitting in his luxurious cabin doing some work on his computer; his cabin was so splendid that anyone who comes in did not go without praising it, costliest furniture and designed by world known interior designers.

He had a habit of always wearing a Bluetooth in ear and a smart watch in his hand.

Mr. Datt comes in the cabin and says-"Sir, all preparations have been done.

As you want, the insurance firm should be named after your father, so tomorrow is the opening ceremony of our insurance firm, RIMA (Rudra Insurance Management Arm)."

Samrat is in with all smile, and then in an earnest style he says-"You are the person whom I can trust. Many have came in life, but no faithful and capable person like you has ever been seen. Really, you are unique; my father did right by choosing you as his associate, if you were not there, who would handle all this."

"Sir, that was the kindness of your father, he had just supported me when I was going through a very difficult period.I cannot repay the favors in this birth which he has done on me.

And because of the good deeds you have done, I want to always be by your side. Sir, you can trust me completely, I will never let your trust be broken."

"You will never break my trust, that's why I have told you many secrets only. I trust you more than myself and if you left us, I would not be able to take this empire too far. Your presence in this firm is as important as my presence in this firm. Both of us are the wheels because of which this firm has reached so far today. If a single wheel goes out, someone else will overtake us."

He immediately stands up and embraces Mr. Datt tightly-"You have supported me a lot, never leave me."

Both have moist eyes...

Then Mr. Datt says-"Sir, keep your trust on me, I'll not be my ability reduced at all and I will dedicate wholeheartedly to the growth of this firm."

After Datt leaves, Samrat wipes his moist eyes with his handkerchief and turns his chair to the glass side of the building.

A remembrance flashed, the past due to which he has been able to sit in that chair today.

It was 1994;

A Ford car stops outside 'Singh Broking Solutions'; a man wearing a brand new suit steps out of the car. The man was none other than the 26-year-old Samrat. The guard standing at the building's gate greets him and opens the door for him. Then he stops an employee and asks where is his boss's cabin; that employee gives the way of cabin and also says that you cannot meet him without an appointment so on this, Samrat asks him if he wants to meet his boss, whom will he has to meet first?

He then arrives at the reception desk, when the receptionist keeps looking at him; giving her the glad eye, he says-"My appointment was fixed with your boss."

"Let me check sir...

Have you come from 'McHattson Motors'?"

"Yes"

"Well you arrived 15 minutes early, but the boss is free now, so you can meet him.

Your name please?"

Pausing for a while, he says in a solemn accent-"By the way, I am the CIO of 'McHattson Motors' and I really don't know who has to come to give this presentation. The CTO sent me in his place at the last moment and my name is Samrat.

Do you have any problem now?"

She is getting confused that might she allow him to go in the cabin or not but there is a CIO of a big motor company in front of her, how can she refuse him.

He again says-"I don't have much time, can I meet your boss right away. Your boss has said that he wants to see this presentation today."

"Okay, you may go sir."

Standing at the door, she asks to her boss-"Sir, CIO of 'McHattson Motors' wants to meet you?"

The owner of the 'Singh Broking Solutions', Rudra Pratap Singh says-"Okay, let him in."

He asks him to sit and waits for his presentation but Samrat is quiet. After waiting for some time, Rudra says-

"So, which presentation you want to show?"

"I'm not what you are thinking."-Samrat says very gravely.

Gazing up him, he says-"So, if you are not, what I'm thinking. Who are you?"

Both are looking at each other and both are remain silent; after a while Samrat says-"Actually, I'm a genie; I save people from troubles and fulfill their wishes."

"Sorry, I didn't understand."

Samrat smirked-"Yes, you heard it right. I save people from their difficulties and fulfill their wishes."

"So, do you understand, I'm in a difficulty?"

"Yes, and I can save you from that difficulty, from which no one can save you except me."

Rudra Pratap now becomes serious-"Keep saying, as soon as you stop, I'll call security."

Then showing an ID card Samrat says-"I'm agent of Intelligence Bureau. I was spying at Eastern Bank a few days ago; there is a huge scam in that bank of approximates Rs. 185 Crores. Which will be announced to the public after 2 days from today and I get to know that you have 1.03% stakes of that bank. And if you will not sell those shares by tomorrow then you'll be ruined."

Rudra gives a sly look on him-"Okay, now it's my turn...security, come into my cabin."-he says through intercom.

Eastern bank was one of the top 10 banks of India and everyone was ready all the time to bidding in high price. And in such a situation, no one would want to sell so much shares of this bank to someone else due to any kind of rumors.

Samrat realizes that he will be thrown out of this office shortly, he stares at him and he quickly says-"Exactly 6 months ago, you blackmailed a major holding partner of Eastern Bank, Mr. Tatva Sinha and got 0.78% stakes of that bank to your dear friend Prana Singh. And what did Sinha sell so many shares through blackmail, I have that videoclip. Only three people knew this thing."

It is said that the door of the cabin opens suddenly, and that scared receptionist stands at the door with a man in black suit and red tie-"Sorry sir, the one sitting in front of you is not the CIO of McHattson Motors, an employee came from there, whose appointment is with you."

But Rudra Pratap is stunned, that thing is running in his mind that only three people knew this secret so how did he get to know the secret of blackmailing.

Both are gazing at each other till then two security guards come inside the cabin and moves toward Samrat. But Samrat's eyes are fixed on Rudra. One of those guards is about to grab Samrat's collar, suddenly Rudra Pratap orders-"Stop." He tells them both to go back and also to the receptionist.

Then he stands up and roaming about him, and moves toward Samrat and says-"So, what is the name of this genie cum Intelligence Bureau agent?"

Samrat gets a little laugh-"Samrat, my name is Samrat. And I'm not an agent of any Intelligence Bureau, that ID card was fake."

"So Mr. Samrat, how did you know about that deal?"

He smiled-"Put to dust on old things...

There is no thinking about past, but keeping the future in mind, up build your present."

"Okay, let's put shit off the past. But how can I trust

the inside news that you have just brought."

He smiled-"The way I came to know about your friend's deal with Tatva Sinha, the same way I came to know about the scam of this bank."

Then Samrat takes out his phone and playing a video clip, he presents it in front of him.

In that video, there is a board meeting of Eastern Bank, where all the board members including the chairman are looking sad. The chairman said to the board members-"After 4 days from today, we will tell about this scam to the SEBI and the police."

Suddenly, Samrat snatches the mobile from his hand.

A specialty of Rudra Pratap was that he was a straight forward person, he smiled and says-"So, what is your benefit in this?"

"Benefit, that will I take by showing the second clip.

For now, I'm going. See you after a few days."

He turns and goes back, and here Rudra Pratap is only beholding him from back.

After 2 days, exactly happened as Samrat had said; the Eastern Bank chairman himself informed the police and media about the scam. This thing spread like a bushfire and further, Eastern Bank's stock plunged 20% before the market closed. Many investors lost crores of rupees. A crowd of investors and traders were ululating that day but only 2 men were happy; the one was Rudra Pratap Singh and another was his friend Prana Singh. Because they were the only people who sold all their stakes of Eastern Bank before the announcement of scam, in this way, those people remained far away from this loss.

5 days after this Bank's share crashed, Samrat reached to the office of Singh Broking Solutions; and this time he

really had an appointment. When Rudra Pratap saw Samrat entering the cabin, he got up from the chair and hugged him-"Come, my genie; you are truly no less than an angle."

Asking him to sit, he asks-"How is doing?"

He says with a little laugh-"I feel like the trunk of a tree that has saved the life of a drowning in the sea."

Both of them laugh loudly and then Rudra Pratap says-"Really, you're such a wonderful guy. If you had not given me that inside information at the right time, I would have been sitting under this table and crying, having lost 167 crores by now.

You came and helped me at the right time; just like an angle. Tell me, what you want?"

"Not much, just 30% of what you have gained."

He smirked and says-"Okay, I'll give you 30%.

But tell me, where will you invest it?"

Before Samrat says something, he says-"In your detective agency?"

Samrat becomes silent just after hearing this because he didn't tell about this thing to Rudra Pratap; he is now waiting to see what Rudra Pratap will say next.

Then Rudra Pratap says-"So Mr. Samrat, your detective agency has solved 13 cases in the last one and a half year; in which you employs some 20 agents. You and all your agents have 6 mobile SIM card and by which you change the ID, you spy. And just like that, you showed me the fake ID of an agent of Intelligence Bureau."

Even after hearing all this, Samrat remains silent but now there is slight smile on his unreadable face. Then Rudra Pratap says again-"Surprised? Knowing from where I got so much information about you...

You're a kid now, how much you know about a businessman...

You are just a baby now, wearing diaper who only knows how to drink milk and the children never walk alone in the highway, otherwise they will be crushed to death."

Samrat was still quiet and staring him just like he is waiting for his turn.

But Rudra Pratap is still solemn-"Till now, you have not made so much money with that little detective firm so that you can afford a Ford car but you came here on that day by booking a Ford car to show off and you wore nice clothes as if you were really an Intelligence Bureau agent.

You're very quiet today; will you not say anything today?"

Samrat is quiet and spinning the paperweight like a peg top and he suddenly says-"Name- Yuga, age- 34 years and height- 6'2" of that agent who has been working for you for the last 12 years. He has a very good relation in every Govt. department so that he can find out any information about anyone."

After saying this, he stops and Rudra Pratap went perturbed on hearing, how he came to know about Yuga. His eyes widened with surprise that Samrat spied him who had gone to spy on him. Before Rudra Pratap says something, looking in the eyes of Rudra Pratap, Samrat says-"So, is he the person not whom you called on the same day at 05:15 PM to spy on me.

And let me tell you one more fact which he does not tell you that he has lost all his hair and he wears wig and he did his health checkup 7 months ago, the doctor told him that he has diagnosed with cancer."

A sly look is on Samrat's face and a kind of fear in the

eyes of Rudra Pratap; things turned around. Rudra Pratap is thinking that how did he know that he made a call to Yuga on that day on 05:15 PM because nobody knew this thing except him and also how the hell he got to know about the medical history of Yuga.

"How did you know all this?"-Rudra Pratap asked.

"I have said it before and I'm saying again it...

Put to dust on old things."-he replied with a grin on his face.

Angry Rudra Pratap now stands-"No, this time, you have to tell me that how the hell did you know that...

Otherwise, I'll put you in jail for tapping my phone; then you have to teach all your strategy to your cellmates."

"Just relax Mr. Rudra; I didn't tap your mobile.

Actually, sitting here you were talking so loudly to Yuga, that I heard easily, nothing else."

He is still staring Samrat because both people know that on that day there was no one else in the office except for Rudra Pratap.

Then smiling over him, he finally bowed on the anger of Rudra Pratap. He takes that paperweight which he was spinning. Looking carefully at that paperweight, he is smiling and says-"Microphone"

Rudra snatches that paperweight from his hand and throws away it through the window. He moves toward Samrat and warns him that this thing should not be done again. And then he calmed his temper but he has not much confidence as he has before.

The air is cleared now; then Samrat says-"And the thing was to come here by Ford car, so if I had not done so, instead of saluting me, the guard of your office would have stopped me."

"You're very cleaver."

"But you have said true that now I'm a suckling child and if I walk alone on the highway, big cars will crush me to death. Therefore I need a support so I can walk on his coattails.

I need a Godfather to be firmly established myself in this industry."

Both are gazing at each other in their eyes and Rudra is sensing what he wants to say.

"You know Samrat; I wanted my son to be such sharp minded as you are, his thinking should be such as you have.

But maybe out of perquisite, I gave free rein to him. He started spending my money in his wantonness. He doesn't value money at all. I explained to him many times that if you don't value money, money will not value you; but he never tried to understand this.

But I like you very much; would that you were be my son so that I never care about the future of my brand name.

I also came to know that you are an orphan...

So, will you be my son? I wanna adopt you."

A smile come across his face-"You know that I'm an orphan but perhaps you don't know that my parents did not have the money to keep me alive, so they left me in an orphanage. Childhood has spent by in penury, I have seen many dangerous turns in my life in every step. But maybe God wanted me to become a pure gold by heating up in fire and one day be crafted into a marvelous piece by a goldsmith like you. It will be my pleasure to call you Dad. I saw a dream that I'll be very rich and it is said that *if you want something with full devotion, then the whole universe kneels in front of your persistence* and see, universe arranged such that today I and you are going to build relation of father and son."

Just then, the door opens and Mr. Datt comes in-"Congratulations sir, that half-murder charge was leveled against you, today the judge has acquitted you."

He stands up and moves toward a table near to him-"I had to win; after all, I had much greased the palm of the judge...

So Samrat, this is the power of money."

Popping the cork of a Brut Champagne, he makes three flutes-"But anyway, we should celebrate the victory."

When he hands Datt a flute of champagne, he refused to drink, then Rudra Pratap says-"This is not just for today's victory, I'm offering you this for all those victories in which you supported me wholeheartedly.And probably, I am the luckiest person in the industry that I have a secretary like you. If you had not been with me, I wouldn't have won those so many wars. You're my strategus who supports me at every step and who never let me defeated. You are the only person in the world whom I can trust completely. You are the only one who can understand; what I want. You're such a terrific guy, Datt. You are one of the 1% of the loyal and honest secretaries of the world.

Because I know many businessmen whose secretaries betrayed.

But you are a man of word who can do anything for his commitment."

Datt's eyes become moist because he did not get so much love and respect from anyone else, Rudra's family considers Datt a part of his family and his family has also given full support in thick and thin of Datt.

"Never forsake us"-Rudra Pratap says with moist eyes.

"You don't need to say that. How can I forsake you?

And my entire birth will be spent in paying off the favor of what you have done for me. And if you had not helped me during that time of trouble, when would I have committed suicide. Today I'm alive because of you; that is why I have devoted myself wholeheartedly to you."

Samrat is surprised but smiling.

After some time, Rudra Pratap picks up another flute of Champagne and moves toward Samrat–"C'mon Samrat, this is time for double celebration."

Then Datt asks–"Double celebration?"

"Yes Datt, double celebration...

He is Samrat, and I'm gonna adopt him. He is going to be my son.

Now after me, only Samrat and Indra will take over this empire."

"Not only will take over but will enlarge"–Samrat said.

Both Samrat and Rudra laugh at this but having a grin on face, Datt is astounded on this decision because this will make huge impact on the industry. *No king wants his empire to have more than one pretender thereafter*, then how did Rudra take such a big decision so soon.

After some time, Samrat says to Rudra Pratap–"I wanna talk to you in private."

After Datt leaves, Samrat says–"How do you trust this secretary Datt so much?

You are a businessman and you know better that no one can be trusted in case of money. How did you give him such relaxation in case of money?

Rather, you should trust him who is powerful in every aspect. On whose head, the crown of power and honor as like you have."

Smirking at him, he utters-"Samrat, now you're going to be my son; so, what I'm going to tell you is to consider it as the key to success in life. And I have not even told this mantra to my son Indra and you also should not tell this to anyone...

In this world, you should not trust anyone except yourself. In your life or even in your business, never trust anyone. But you should keep on assuring them that you trust them with all your heart."

"Oh...wow, so this is the secret of your success, by which you have built a great empire...

But what is the secret behind keeping the person in the illusion?

Then he smiled-*"History is witness that the person who has the avarice for power or money does not belongs to anyone, such a person is not trustworthy at all. And the thing is to convince someone that you trust with closed eyes, because of this his loyalty towards you increases.*

Many times in life, we need loyalty, not the crown, to move forward and loyalty can neither be bought nor forcefully imposed on anyone. Loyalty can be won by expressing love to the people. The frightened heads which are bowed in with our power stand up first for the rebellion but those who bow down to our loyalty and friendship, are ready to be the first to be cut in times of trouble."

Samrat is now blissed out inwardly by this past and thinking that he has built such a huge empire today, following the mantra of success given by his Godfather that no one has the power to demolish such a huge fortress wall.

☐☐☐

FIVE

"There is no way to live other than intrepidity, the throb of your heart should be like a clangor of conch-shell of a war. There must be thumping and unblushing yearning to come to the best in the path of success. So much yearning that whatever you ask for, universe present that thing to your feet."

\- Samrat Singh 'Sikandar'

After 3 weeks;

While many businessmen monitored their company's monthly growth, Samrat used to check weekly growth reports because he strongly believes that *if success is not achieved at the right time, it will not be a true success,* that's why he keeps increasing his speed and work capacity in every step, perhaps this was the reason he had achieved such a huge success in a very short period of his time.

So, after 3 weeks he was monitoring growth report of his joint venture insurance, 'Rudra Insurance Management Arm (RIMA)' but he found negative result instead of enormous operational expenditure.

On seeing this, he orders his secretary Datt-"Come with me immediately to the Management Arm."

"But sir, only 3 weeks have passed; wouldn't it to be too early to go there and scold them?"

"I'm not going for scold them"-then Samrat wears his

goggles-"Datt, *who are aware of small things often escape from great destruction.*"

Both people reach RIMA, he picks up the mike from reception table and he ingresses into the office-"Listen everyone..."

He moves towards the dais-"Answers my questions..."

All the employees leave their work and get closer to the dais.

He tells that he wants to hear all the answers in unison roar-"What is needed to rule this world?"

All the employees started looking at each other and then they say in unison-"POWER"

And then Samrat started roaring-"*There are only two types of people in this world - The Ruler and The Slave. First is one who has power and the second is one who lives in fear.*

The Rulers rule those people who are scared and afraid of walking on the corridors of power and those who are slaves deny this fear, run away from this fear and those who draw a veil over their fears; this universe punishes them that they always have to be remain in their fears.

All the dreams and desires of that scared slave are reduced to ashes and he lives as a slave all his life.

If you get a chance, would you like to become a ruler or a slave?"

Thunderous applause in the office and this generates vibes in the atmosphere; every employee gets excited and charged and they roar-"The Ruler..."

"So, what you will choose – The Power or The Fear?"

"The Power..."-employees said in unison.

Then Samrat says-"*There is no way to live other than*

intrepidity, the throb of your heart should be like a clangor of conch-shell of a war. There must be thumping and unblushing yearning to come to the best in the path of success. So much yearning that whatever you ask for, universe present that thing to your feet."

He comes down from the dais-*"When a lion is hungry, he comes out of his cave; therefore you must have appetite for power and money. Your performance to work should be such that the rest of your competitor gets frightened by the way you work like a thunderous roar of a lion shivers all the animals of the forest. Success loves speed, and the terrible the appetite, the faster will be the speed."*

All employees go spellbound, Samrat again says-*"The game will go on, the question is- does the world play with you or do you play with the world..."*

"We..."

"Your progress and destruction are in your own hands. If you will be like the rest of the people, then your consequences will be like those...

A person who is satisfied with a small amount of money, money abandons them.

Hence, go and make this insurance firm of the richest agents in the world."

Samrat has filled his agents with a great enthusiasm with his thoughts. He wins over his all employees by his thinking.

This matter also reaches Gajendra; he realizes that he made no mistake by befriending Samrat. But now is the time to tell whether his decision was right or not.

Two months have passed; everything was going well in Gajendra's life. And also delighted to see the unexpectedly exponentially growth of that joint venture insurance firm. And an additional goodness was that he had invested heavily in a pharmaceutical company, which stocks did not have much demand in the market but Gajendra knows that after five weeks there will be a tremendous growth in the stock price of that company. The reason behind this is that the pharma company had been working in its lab for the last 5 years on a medicine that can help a drug addict to get rid of drugs in just 3 months. And the name of that pharma company is 'Homoss Pharmaceuticals'. Such medicine is coming in the market, whose demand is very high all over the world. The number of drug addicts is increasing and everyone wants his friend to get rid of the drug addiction. For this, he will also be willing to pay the price asked for that medicine. Trials of this medicine were going on through illegal methods on humans, for this reason, the rest of the world know nothing about it. Trials were in last phase and had just 5 weeks left for the result.

Sitting in his cabin, Gajendra is reading a newspaper and he saw news that 'CLC Pharma ltd.' has patented a medicine 2 days ago, who claims to have get rid of any form of addictive drug. And because of this news, the share price of the companies in the pharma sector has upsurge a lot; and the share price of CLC Pharma ltd. are soaring, only increasing, everyone wants to buy it.

On reading this, Gajendra departs towards the lab of Homoss Pharma; so after going there, he gets to know that the hard drives of all the computers have been stolen and all the computers have been burnt, all the equipments and chemicals are spreading out on the ground in the lab. Formulas and chemicals made after five years of hard work are missing, maybe stolen. All the scientists are weeping and wailing that their hard work of five years has ruined.

They have no proof that the medicine which was patented by CLC Pharma, actually it is the hard work of Homoss Pharmaceutical's scientist. And CLC Pharma steals that formula and patented to its name.

Gajendra returns from there and sits in his chair desperate and thinking that the five years of hard work of scientists has ruined but also his Rs. 70 Crores got squandered. This was such a huge loss that it is not easy to compensate because this need lot of time to earn this wealth from the stock market.

Then suddenly, Kavish asks to come in the cabin; and he was going to present portfolio growth of this month but Gajendra suddenly added that he has a loss of Rs. 70 Crores and he further adds-"I didn't tell anyone about this except Salila and all the scientists working in that lab were keep being closely watched. This was a hole-and-corner experiment; don't know how the information about this leaked out. The thieves were so vicious that they did not leave a single proof so that we can prove that CLC Pharma is a thief and a fraud company. Do not know who is behind all this?"

"I know who is he?"-a voice from a man standing at the door of the cabin.

When Gajendra looks there, he saw that Samrat's stepbrother Indra Singh is standing there. He was a little surprised; because he just knew him only by profession.

Gajendra says-"Do you know, what we're discussing about here?"

He sits and tells that he wants to talk with him in private. After Kavish leaves, Gajendra waits for Indra to speak.

Then Indra says-"I know that you have just lost your Rs. 70 Crores, by Homoss Pharmaceuticals."

Gajendra's ears pricked up because no one knew this thing-"How did you know that?"

"I also know that the Homoss Pharma was working in

such a medicine that can help the drug addicts to get rid of drugs, from last 5 years.

And that formula was stolen just a few days ago; and 2 days ago CLC Pharma has patented the same formula in its name. But you guys have not a single evidence to prove that this formula is result of your hard work."

"How did you know that?"-this time anger is reflecting in his face.

"Look, pay attention to what I'm going to say..."-then Indra throws a file which he brought, in front of Gajendra-"This is the disclosure of shareholdings of CLC Pharma."

Gajendra picked up that file and starts reading, suddenly Indra says-"Just 15 days ago, Samrat bought 6% stakes in CLC Pharma. It means he knew that there is going to be a lot of demand of that medicine in the market.

Now just think, when this theft happened a few days ago, then how did Samrat knew this thing 15 days ago that Homoss Pharma is making a medicine which formula will be stolen. And CLC Pharma will patent that formula in its name."

For Gajendra, this was really surprising that on what reason Samrat invested in that CLC Pharma. This formula has been stolen, this means that the conspiracy of this theft was preparing for the last 15 days.

"What you want to say, call a spade a spade..."-the loss of Rs. 70 Crores to Gajendra has been greatly hurted-"Look, I know very well that you and Samrat do not get on well with each other. You guys are just brothers only in the eyes of people.

Do you want to trap him because of that enmity?"

"I knew that you will think such...

Okay, let me tell you one thing, about one month

before today, you left your home for Homoss Pharma's lab at 02:00 AM at night."

Gajendra is shocked but he agrees, then Indra further says-"Then the insiders of that bloody Samrat was following you; that insiders who work in your firm."

This thing came as a bolt from the blue for Gajendra. He had no idea of this.

Then Indra again says-"Yes, the insiders of Samrat are not only in your firm but they are in the many stock firms of Mumbai and perhaps they are in many small and big companies; and they use to give inside news to Samrat. And on the basis of those inside news, his firm is now in the top 5 stock firms of India."

Gajendra is still stunned; he is completely taken aback from this-"How did you know all this?"

"My one insider is working with his broking solutions for the last one year. These days she has came very close to him; and he blurt out all these things last night, in a drunken state.

She kept on asking and he kept on telling. He became besotted with her. Till yesterday, the secret which only Samrat and his secretary Datt knew, he easily told my insider, Yati.

But he didn't know that he was telling his enemies his weakness."

"How can I believe these things of yours?"

"I know you're a businessman and a businessman doesn't take decision on rumors."-Indra replied-"By the way, you must have heard the name of Aryendra Chauhan."

Gajendra agrees that he knows him who is the Joint Director of department of investigation of ED.

Then Indra says-"I have come to know that he wants

to expose Samrat. He will help me find evidence against Samrat, then you will easily believe on me. Now I'm going to rub shoulders with him; because he hates Samrat as much as I hate him. And I'll take advantage of this hatred to destroy Samrat."

"I met Samrat, I know him very well. He is damn terrific businessman. One day while talking to him, I also felt for a moment that he must have come for his some kind of expedience; but I fell into his illusion trap.

If all this is done by him, he will see my vengeance. I will blow him out of the water. Pretending to be a friend, he threw a dagger in my back.

I'll never let off him...

Okay, but tell me one thing, I already knew that you hated your step-brother a lot but how much hate does the empire that Samrat has expanded, which is basically your father's legacy, you want to ruin it. If Samrat will be ruined, your father's name will also be ruined."

"Yes Mr. Rai, I hate him very much and his perishment will only harm him, not the empire."

"Why, I didn't understand?"-Gajendra surprised.

"In fact, my father had made a will that if one of their two sons goes astray, so to expand the company, all his inheritance will be that of another son.

That is why till today I have not tried to kill him, I just want to destroy his brand name.

And in reality, which is my father's legacy is not someone else's right, but my right."

"Don't worry, perhaps he has not yet been confronted with any real highborn businessman, if you will prove that Samrat is behind all this, together we will ruin him."-Gajendra was basically aggressive in nature, even he does not get anything by taking revenge but he definitely used to teach his enemy a lesson.

The friendship between Gajendra and Indra was intended only and only to ravage Samrat. *The enemy of our enemy is our friend;* perhaps due to this thinking, he approached Gajendra. Now, his next move was to befriend one another enemy of Samrat, who is Aryendra Chauhan.

Aryendra also easily become a friend of Indra. But perhaps Indra had forgotten one thing- *of policemen, neither friendship is good nor enmity.* Because Aryendra's job was to capture fraudsters; whoever proved a fraudster, Aryendra will seize him by the throat- now whether he is Samrat or Indra or the stock market king, Gajendra Rai.

SIX

*"There is a specialty of deception that often
that traitor was our friend"*

– Gajendra Rai

After ten days;

Aryendra gets to know from his secret agent that Samrat is going to meet some of his insiders at 01:30 PM in a nightclub today. Aryendra didn't tell anyone about it, neither his colleagues nor Indra and Gajendra. And he went alone to that nightclub.

There he saw that Samrat was going towards the roof of that nightclub; where on these days, no one comes because of the construction. And Aryendra is sneaking up behind Samrat; Samrat is walking ahead and Aryendra at a distance of about six feet.But suddenly Samrat stops and turns; he saw that Aryendra is standing in front.

Then Aryendra says-"So, today my wish for years has come to an end. Today, I caught you red handed with your insider."

There is a dead silence to prevail in the air; both are staring at each other.

Then after some time, Samrat says-"So now, will you arrest yourself....?"

Suddenly both started laughing at loud and Aryendra

utters-"How are you, my friend?"

Tony startled-"What? Aryendra called Samrat his friend?...

But he was his enemy, you told. And you have said that by hook or by crook, he wanted to expose Samrat. And the utterance of Aryendra that the enemy should never know how much enmity you have with him.

So how does all this change? When did they become friends?

When?"

His grandpa has a grinning face-"Actually, there was no enmity between them...

It was Samrat who told Aryendra to do that; so that world understand that Aryendra wants to expose Samrat.

So that when Samrat's enemies come to him, Samrat will get about it, which of his enemy is plotting against him at this time.

The truth was that Samrat had chosen Aryendra to arrange contact with his insiders from every company. So that if any insider gets caught red handed, then Aryendra will take responsibility in defence of him that he is not any insider but a secret agent of him.

This is the reason why any insider of Samrat never gets caught.

The same insiders used to send information to Aryendra as well, with the help of which he could solve any case within a month.

Today he has been able to achieve the top position in his department by dint of the insiders of Samrat; and in return, Samrat used to expose his enemies through

Aryendra."

"So, he was a bogus super cop, just a sycophant of Samrat?"

"Yes, my dear grandson, all this was the ploy of Samrat.

Samrat was well wont with the ways by which he could send his snoopers into the camps of his enemies."

"Oh My God! What a man! Means there was no such slackness in a place that the enemy could enter his fort."

"Not a bit of slackness...that makes him Samrat Singh 'Sikandar'.

When he had set up his insiders everywhere, how could he miss out the police department? For this reason, he has no fear of the police until he obliterates all evidences of the fraud he has done. And in this way, one by one he was going to win wars by deploying a tremendous soldier on every battledore.

So when they both hug each other, Samrat says-"So friend, why you call me here?"

"I called Samrat Singh 'Sikandar' to warn him that one who has made not a single mistake till today, now he has made a blunder...

Your step-brother Indra wants to destroy you. And Gajendra Rai has also got to know that your insiders brings the inside news of his firm to you. And you became such a big investor of India by dint of those insiders. And since he found out that you have made loss of his Rs. 70 Crores, he wants to squandered you completely.

All your enemies have made friendship with each

other so that together they will take revenge from you."

"Don't worry, my dear"-Samrat has a grinning face-"This is all a part of my plan.

I knew that Indra sent that girl and therefore I'm playing with her. Only the information that I wanted has reached them."

Aryendra flabbergasted with this because until now he had not told about that agent of Indra, about whom Indra had already told Aryendra, when he came to befriend him-"Oh my goodness! That's why I thought till today, not even a single mistake was made by you, so how could you make such a blunder...

Really my friend, you're great; nobody has mind like you in this world.

So, you already knew about that girl, whose name maybe Yati, is an agent of your step-brother Indra?"

Samrat replied with a grin on his face-"Yes, when my insiders have reached more than 70% of several sectors of companies of India, then how can I forget my dear brother Indra."

"Umm...you are amazing.

So tell me, what's next?"

"By the way, I know Indra; he must be keeping his eye on you too. So, listen to me, understand one thing very well that from now you will not come to meet me nor try to make any kind of contact.

And go on doing what my brother says. Envy has been in his heart for so many years; I think there must be terrible conspiracies against me are running in his mind.

Anyway, my two insiders are in the firm of Gajendra, they will give all the inside information to me. But if someone gets see you with me, then the whole game will be spoiled."-Samrat comes close to Aryendra and puts his hand on his shoulder-"Aryendra, you helped me a lot. Really, my fortune is so good that a true and loyal friend like you is written in my destiny. You always supported me on time and have never left me in the midstream...

Thank you very much my dearest friend. Be with me forever."

Aryendra with moist eyes-"My friend, if you had not helped me at the right time and if you would not supported me with your insider army, I might not be able to reach such a highest designation. It was not me who helped you, but that is you who helped me every time; I have to express thanks."

Then they hug each other, by promising that they will not meet until Samrat says to meet.

After some days;

Sitting in his car, Gajendra Rai leaves his home at 01:00 AM in night. Through going on dead silence paths, he stops his car at rear gate of an arms factory. A man receives him and takes him in that factory.

A man was following stealthily Gajendra's car from his home to that factory.

Perhaps again this time Gajendra has made such an investment in huge amount in a company, which can give him lots of profit in a short time.

That snooper also reached that arms factory by following him. When that man peeks in secretly, he gets to know that Gajendra has invested Rs. 87 Crores in that arms factory and that company is working on a gun that will pierce all the impenetrable and strong metal in front of the dangerous laser light that will come out from that gun. And when this gun lands in a war, it can defeat entire enemies in a day. That man returns from there only after hearing this and sitting on his bike he reaches a ruins, Madh Fort far away. The man meets another man in that ruins and he tells him that it must to tell the Colonel that tonight, king went to an arms factory at 01:30 AM, where they were talking about a laser gun which can burn the entire army of enemy to the ashes in a day.

Then suddenly the sound of plaudit is heard; when both of them look back, they give a start, because that applause was playing none other than the owner of Rai Securities Limited, Gajendra Rai, and standing next to him was Indra, the step-brother of the owner of Singh Broking Solutions.

And when Gajendra saw both of them, he stops clapping because that two were none other than his employees; one of them was Mahidhar and another was his most loyal employee, Kavish. Both of them started job together at Gajendra Securities Ltd. and both were also strong contenders for the company's 'Broker of the year' award.

Gajendra gets very angry after seeing Kavish because he trusted him a lot. Gajendra gave Kavish a smack across the face-"So, you are the bloody traitor. You cheat....you said that you will never break my trust and you will work day and night for our firm; and you'll destroy the enemies...

Where is your firm promises?..."-he said with a flinch.

Kavish fallen from his favor, lowering his eyes he is hearing all this. But then after a while, he started smiling-"Hey boss, I promised to crush the enemies to the dirt but you have turned hostility with us."

Gajendra grabbed him by the shirt collar-"So, Samrat had sent both of you in my firm and you were told Samrat about that secret deal...

But still I can't believe it; because my agents were following you for almost a week, who had spied all over you. So how did you avert from his eyes?"

Kavish removes Gajendra's hand from his collar-"I knew that as Durjay did with you, like that I would not come out as a traitor, you will put your agents for spying on me.

So, all I had to do a drama, in which I had to make a fake family so that you could trust me blindly.

Durjay was also an insider like us; but when he was caught, we had to move further cautiously."

Indra started clapping. He comes in front and says-"That was a good drama. So to catch you, we also had to do a drama so that we can capture all the insiders of Samrat. And see, we caught you...

Now he can't escape. Today, we got hold of his fatal mistake and now he will behind the bars and I will rule on the entire empire."

Then with laughing out loud, Mahidhar comes in front-"But boss, you will never be able to prove any link between us and Samrat Singh 'Sikandar' and nor we will ever give a statement that we work for our colonel Samrat."

These things were going that suddenly the siren of the police jeep is heard.

After some time, joint director of ED Aryendra Chauhan comes in with some policemen. Indra had called Aryendra with some other police officers but he had not told Aryendra that he had set up a trap to capture the two insiders of Samrat.

When Aryendra got to know about this whole thing, then he is thinking that Samrat has already told about those two insiders but he has also said that whatever his brother will say, Aryendra has to do the same. Now he is in a dilemma as to whether to put insiders in jail or not; because this time he can't save them both by saying that these are secret agents of police. And if he captures them, then the plan made by Samrat will be destroyed.

Then suddenly Indra speaks-"Why're you standing, put them behind the bars and take statement from them that they're insiders of Samrat. And drag him by the collar into the prison. After all, this is your wish too."

After a while, Aryendra says to his police officers to capture them and then beckons to Indra and Gajendra for talk in private; when three of them would go a little bit away from there, Aryendra says-"You guys, listen to me carefully; if they don't speak out, then we will never be able to prove that Samrat is behind many stock market scam, so he will never be captured.

And suppose, if they blurted that they're working for Samrat; even then, due to no link and no strong evidence between them and him, Samrat will be easily get away from this. Because you must have known that the businessman has so much power that he can get acquitted in such small cases in a snap, even then you will not be able to harm him.

And in both these cases, if we filed FIR that they're the insiders of Samrat and they give inside news to Samrat, even we will not be able to prove the allegations easily, but by then Samrat will be become more argus-eyed.

And you guys do not take him easy, he is not so stupid. He must have made some ways to escape from all this; after all he is a damn dangerous business tycoon."

Gajendra and Indra are assessing the all circumstances that even by capturing these two; they will not be able to do much harm to Samrat. Both made a nod on this, Gajendra says-"You're right. Capturing these two will make Samrat more cautious and he will get to know that we together are plotting to take the empire away from him."

Then Indra interjects-"But even leaving both of them will be our set back because they will inform Samrat that his all enemies came together."

Then Aryendra says-"Don't be worry, I'll put these two in prison in some other charges and if then Samrat tried to contact both of them then we get strong evidence against him."

All three agree on this and Aryendra arrests them in another charge and takes them to the police car to put them into jail.

After leaving Aryendra and the police officers, only two people were standing there- Gajendra Rai and Indra Singh. Then Indra says-"So, step one of our plan was very successful; we removed the insiders of Samrat from amidst ways, which was our biggest problem. And now it is time, the grime named Samrat has to be eradicated. He troubled me a lot."

As soon as he said that, his glances to fall on that glowing golden watch in the darkness of that night, so he adds-"Hey Rai, I have always seen this watch in your hands. I wanted to praise many times but often forgot. It looks too expensive."

Smiling, Gajendra lifts up that hand-"By the way, I'm fond of expensive watches since long ago and it is the most expensive watch ever of worth Rs. 80,000 which is laced with diamond, gold and platinum."

Indra expresses praise on that watch, then Gajendra says with a smile on his face-"Do you want to know, who has given me this...your brother Samrat."

"Why?"-Indra asked.

"To take advantage from me, it was necessary for him to be in friendship with me. Behind that Insurance Management Arm, he wanted the brand name of me, the stock market king...

So as a first keepsake of that friendship, he gave it to me as a gift.

But now he doesn't know that this watch now reminds me of this enmity. *There is a specialty of deception that often that traitor was our friend.* That's why he came to me for intimacy but now this friend will take advantage of this friendship and cheat him and will slam him where he started to cognizing the life.

Interest in a war is as interesting is our enemy...

It's gonna be very thrilling, Samrat..."

"Samrat...I'll ravage you completely,"

After some time, Indra starts beholding at Gajendra. Gajendra also gets into thinking that why Indra is seeing him like this. Then Indra says-"Rai, do you remember one thing you said, after loss in Homoss Pharma?"

"What?"

"Remember, you have said that if all this is done by Samrat then he will see your vengeance, you will blow him out of the water..."

"Yes, so what?"-he didn't get him, what he intends to say.

Indra becomes taciturnity perhaps something is running in his mind that can fulfill his dream of demolishing Samrat.

Gajendra asked-"What is in your mind?"

"I'm thinking of him whose name is enough to stimulate terror in the hearts of people. Due to that terror, people supplicate that their dwelling might not come in the hurricane of his obstinacy...

I'm thinking of the person who, if he decided to climb the mountain, he would not only reach the apex of that mountain first, but would throw the person who is on his way into the ditch."

Gajendra becomes mildly afraid that about whom Indra is talking about; that name is about to enter his mind, till then a word comes out of Indra's mouth-"THE BUSINESS GOD"

Traces of fear on Gajendra's face and he retreats a few steps out of fear because Indra really uttered the name of the person who is now the most dangerous person of the world. That name is too high for any brand; people were afraid that they might not say something wrong about 'The Business God' on any platform even accidentally otherwise Business God will exterminate him with his whole existence. Whoever wrangled with 'The Business God', soon they have seen as bankrupt and wandering in street like pixilated. Even if Business God had done some harm to some of people, none of them would have dared to say anything bad about The Business God; The Business God had given those people the right to only to observe mourning. The Business God is also a kind of a businessman but he is such a dangerous businessman that trusting him is as if blindfolded and walking on a rope tied at two ends of a trench; but there have been many people in history who have performed such miracle and they have enough money to afford 'The Business God' as a business consultant.

People are looking for opportunity but Business God is not an indigent of any opportunity, he has won the whole world on his own prerequisites. The terror of devastation caused by The Business God is ingrained very well in the hearts of people and for this reason, he easily rules over these bowed heads. He believes that our enemy concedes defeat when he realizes his weaken condition. And it is pleasure to conquer when we force the enemy to kneel down in his own barton.

The Business God is like that berserk lion rambling on the forest, who has the power, courage and intrepidity to perish even the biggest brutes in the dust.

The fear is reflected in Gajendra's face and the dead silence to prevail in that ruins-"You probably have no idea how dangerous that person is, otherwise you would not have been able to utter his name so easily."

"I have heard the tidings of wreaked havoc by him, even felt it.

But he is the only one in this world who can help us to take revenge; he is the only personality who can support us then we can throw Samrat from his throne to the streets."

Gajendra then admonishes to him-"But you don't know that trusting that person is absurdity because if Samrat offered more money than us, he would be easily of him. And if both of them come together, then both of us will be bankrupted with money and from dignity, even they will together rob the whole world."

"You're right...but this will not happen."-Indra gave a sly look to him.

"How can you say this?"

"You don't know my step-brother, but I know him...I'm well acquainted with his attitude. One of the specialties of Samrat is that he is not afraid of anyone and if we use this specialty to our advantage?"

But Gajendra is still confused, what Indra wants to say.

Then Indra says-"When The Business God will cause a loss to Samrat; then it will be first time for Samrat when he will be defeated and this defeat will hurt his ego a lot, he will not suffer this defeat. And by getting angry he will definitely give an open challenge to The Business God, which will become the biggest mistake of his life because it is the tenet of Business God that whoever has raised his voice against him, Business God has dissipated him totally; so that he can tell everyone how dangerous it can be to mess with The Business God.

So all we have to do is wait till that blunder of Samrat, after that Business God will do all thing on his own. We will just have to sit and watch the combat between these two. This will be a battle in which two people will definitely fight among themselves but we will benefit. And after that open challenge of Samrat, we can be fully composed that The Business God will never support Samrat. After that we can fully trust The Business God."

Gajendra made a nod on this and praises his sagaciousness-"The first defeat of Samrat must be so huge that he shouts in pain; and in anger, he made that mistake, which thought of consequences is enough to scare the people.

Then both of them return to their home, by deciding that now The Business God will have to be brought into this battle because he is the only one, whomever he supports, the battle will in his account and then his monopoly in that area is established.

❑❑❑

SEVEN

"People become so outrage in the blaxe of vengeance that they don't even know that they are blazing themselves first in that blaxe."

- The Business God

After 16 days;

Indra enters in the cabin of Gajendra Rai, and smiling, sits in front of him. Seeing Indra smiling so much, Gajendra asked the reason. Then Indra says-"Got it."

"What?"-Gajendra wondered.

"Business God's whereabouts..."

Open-mouthed astonishment is on the face of Gajendra, his fingers stopped typing; he is just staring Indra-"It takes two months for any businessman to contact The Business God, and you found out his whereabouts in just half a month."

"Where there is a will, there is a way. I tried much to meet him and God did something that the way to reach him so quickly came to me."

"Which way?"

Indra smiled-"Yesterday a very old friend of mine came to my office to meet me, he wanted the help of Rs. 25 Crores and was refusing to tell me the reason for that money.

After refusing so many times, he took promise from me that I should not tell that thing to anyone, which he was going to tell. Then he told that he had bought a bankrupt nano tech company, 3 years ago; and last year they invent such a mobile battery using nano technology, which can run for one year without charging. After inventing it, he has only Rs. 60 Crores left; which he gave entire to The Business God to achieve monopoly in market. But 4 days ago, Business God suddenly demanded Rs. 25 Crores; so he had to come to me."

"Then?"-Gajendra asked.

"Then what, if he had came to ask me earlier, I would not have given him a single penny but I thought that we also want to deal with The Business God, so if I help him, we can meet Business God soon.

So I helped him on the condition that he will introduce me to The Business God."

"So when he will meet you?"

"He does not meet anyone but people have to go to him to meet.

And that friend will tell about it when and where I can go to meet him. Maybe his message will come soon..."

Now Gajendra feels relax-"You know Indra, *opportunities are available only to those who take right decision at the right time at the right place.* And you made the right decision to help your friend.

Just, this time should not go beyond our cogitation and do not rebel against us. *The existence of Samrat in this world is nothing short of a death for this society and death runs away not from hiding but from facing.* Samrat's hunger for growth has left many hunger-victims.

After some time, he said goodbye to return back to his

office. Getting down from the lift, he steps out of the office and moves towards his Chevrolet car. When he is about to near his car, suddenly he gets a call; call was from an unknown number. When he picks up, Indra gets to hear his friend's voice; this was that friend who asked for Indra's help of Rs. 25 Crores, one day ago. He becomes glad because he feels that Business God has asked him to call to tell me the address and time. And that's exactly what happens; he was told that tomorrow, at 12:00 AM at the Lotus Hotel, The Business God will come in room no. 4910, but the time of The Business God is very valuable, so he will not wait there. So Indra will have to go to that hotel and book that room in his name before reaching him and he has to wait. Indra got that and then he disconnects the phone. Indra becomes very happy as the time of Samrat's ruination draws near.And it seems that the destiny is also in a hurry to ruin Samrat, because it was not possible for anyone to meet Business God so soon.

Indra turns back and stares at the Rai Securities Ltd.; a thought came across his mind that why not give this good news to Gajendra also. Even though The Business God called him alone, but he can tell Gajendra about this; so he moves back to the gate of the building. When he reaches close to the gate, then again he gets a call but this time from different unknown number. He picks up the phone and was about to step inside the gate, by then from the other side of the phone, his friend said-"Do not step inside the gate, sit back in your car and return to your office. If you told this thing to Gajendra Rai or someone else, a havoc of his rage will befall you."

Indra has lifted his leg to step inside the gate, but on hearing this, his step stops there. His friend disconnected the call after saying that but a short of fear is started reflecting in Indra's face. He turns back and looks in all direction but there were only skyscraper buildings, nothing else. He had only thought about telling that thing to Gajendra, so how did Business God know this?

Now Indra gets, why everyone call him The Business God. Today, he felt his power very closely; this frightening experience has trembles him to the inside, that's why people say how harmful is dealings with him.In fright, he sits in his car and returns to his office.

Next day;

He does exactly that, arriving at that hotel half an hour before time, he books the room no. 4910 at his own name. When he stands at the reception, he feels that someone is trying to steal by putting his hand in his pocket; when he turns back with a twitch, he collides with a lady who looks like a business woman. He then squabbled with her; after that he goes to the room no. 4910 and waits for The Business God. And at exactly 11:55 AM, the doorbell of the room rings.

A lady stand in front; Indra is astonished and a little scared because that lady was nobody else but the same with whom he had just had an altercation at the reception. She is just looking at him.

Then Indra gets little scared-"Are you The Business God?"

She replied-"No...Business God is the typhoon which noise is enough to causes people's heart to tremble."

Then suddenly the voice of Tony's mother comes from behind; and she calls him for breakfast. Tony says-"Oh no...momentum breaks."

"No problem...just go and have the breakfast first..."

"Okay...I'll come in few minutes."

After Tony leaves, Tony's grandpa again looks up at the sky and again lost in his days of yore...he is often lost in that pleasing blue ocean.

Suddenly his phone rings...

"Sir, are you there?"

Tony's grandpa says-"Hmm..."

"Sir...the dominion is praying for his warlord.

A devotee has come, taking an offering, who wants God to fulfill his wish."

Tony's grandpa is silent, perhaps he is thinking about something and then he breaks his silence-"Robert, I've always given great heed to pace...

But due to this pace, I've moved far away from my family.

And now I don't want to repeat this mistake again."

"So now has your mind is sated with this game?"

"Whatever be the game, one day mind will be sated...

The honor for which I throw myself into the war, I've bowed it on my own.

But coming at this turn of my life, I've realized that getting respect on the strength of 'Power' is exactly like having the world's most dangerous weapon and realizing that you're the most powerful warrior in the world."

"So far you have told this the only way to get respect and I've learned from you that once you have decided the path, then you shouldn't go away from that path.

Sir, you are The Business God and you have taught me, *the world respects you only when you fight on the battlefield.*"

Today Business God is answerless on this utterance, after all, how can he justify to be unfair his views?

The Business God is now very exhausted of fighting

with everyone, now there is no such zeal in his heart for the sake of which he should return to the field.

He finally breaks his silence-*"Before giving someone a high position and respect, this world wants to ordeal that to what extent he can give proof of his integrity in times of difficulties in the way of protecting the ideal...*

Entire life has passed in an illusion, but now this life is only to protect the ideals.

And by the way, whoever condemn me, I've reduced the existence of all those to ashes."

Robert is silent but in that peace the noise of a storm is being heard-"No sir...you have not yet reduced the existence of all of them in ashes.

A businessman is still swaggeringly around in this world."

It shook up The Business God, after all. Who left now, due to whom The Business God couldn't achieve perfection in his motive-"Who is he?"

"A coal mining merchant, who once used to smuggle gold in Bombay; he has exasperated many traders in coal mining.

And a rival of him has came to me with Rs. 250 Crores, and he wants the monopoly in coal mining."

Business God is quiet, perhaps he is pondering about this, and then Business God says-"Tell him, it will be done."

The man who came out to dominate the entire system, he never knew that because of this he would have to leave his country and settle in any island.

But still The Business God smiles at these things that maybe his life is not over yet that God wants him to do more work now, one more man is yet to be punished for his sins; and that's why he is called The Business God.

Now it's time to get back to the arena.

"Grandpa, I've brought you breakfast"-Tony comes suddenly, and sits in front.

That old fox is just staring his future in him, and maybe that's why he started this story.

Extending hands towards the breakfast, he asks to his grandson-"So, where was I?"

"Hm... Business God is the typhoon which noise is enough to causes people's heart to tremble."-Tony simpered.

"Hm...

As soon as the lady said this, the noise of a helicopter is heard, that sound was coming from the roof of that hotel.

After some time, a man wearing black overcoat with black leather gloves, a black goggles and with a hi-tech Bluetooth enters in the corridor; about six feet brawny figure, behind whom two bodyguards are also entering.

That lady says to Indra-"This is 'The Business God'."

Indra is only gazing at him, a spellbound scene; those are truly lucky who have seen God with their eyes. The Business God came and stands in front of Indra.

Indra quickly puts his hand forward to shake hand with him-"Hello, I'm Indra..."

Even before he says something, The Business God completed his sentence-"I know, son of Godfather...I mean Samrat's Godfather Rudra Pratap Singh."

Indra gets stunned-"Welcome..."

The Business God nods to all of them that they will all

wait outside. Then he enters in the room; and moves toward the window, he started looking the view outside of the window.

Till then Indra closed the door and says-"So The Business God, what's your real name?"

He doesn't look back and remains silent, his eyes is still toward the outside view. Indra is still waiting but Business God doesn't answer his question; perhaps Indra realizes that only the things for which The Business God came here will talk about it and will not answer anything. Indra becomes mildly disappointed and then says-"Your work is to ruin a man."

Saying this, he becomes silent and waits for The Business God to say something. Then Business God turns back and says-"Whom, your step-brother Samrat?"

Indra gets taken aback that how did he knew this. Because he wants to see Samrat ruined, only a few people know this thing, so he asked-"How did you know that?"

The Business God turns back to the window-"God knows everything."

Then he goes ahead to The Business God and says- "From wherever you came to know, it is absolutely true. I want to see ripped to shreds of Samrat's wealth and dignity. Can you do it?"

He turns back with a sly look-"There is nothing that God cannot do."

"So tell me, how much you want oblations?"

"Everything costs in this world and only after paying that cost, you can get that thing.

I use to charge twice as much as my fees for ruining someone."

Indra agrees-"Okay, I'll give you Rs. 170 Crores...

But tell me when and how will you destroy him?"

Then Business God replies-"Till today, no one has understood and nor will ever understand my tactics and conspiracies against the enemy...

Tomorrow wherever you will be, a man named Robert will come to you and will tell you all what things you have to do, okay..."

Indra nodded on this, and then Business God moves toward the door. Then suddenly Indra asked-"By the way, tell me one thing...why you use to charge double fee for ruining someone?"

Business God stops there, he turns back with sedate eyes-*"People become so outrage in the blaxe of vengeance that they don't even know that they are blazing themselves first in that blaxe."*

Indra becomes speechless because this thing was bitter, but also true; and Indra did the same thing. In the blaxe of vengeance for the loss of half of his inheritance, he was ready to pay double the fee to The Business God.

It is said that, a person can even forgive his father's murderer once, but never forgive that one who takes away his ancestral inheritance."

Next day;

Indra reaches Rai Securities Ltd. in his Chevrolet car at 12:00 noon and moves toward the gate of the building, but he suddenly stops and cast of mind that maybe someone is watching him while entering in the building like that day; I can tell all this to Gajendra only if The Business God has assent. He waits for some time there and looking at his phone that maybe he will get the call of The Business God, but this time it doesn't rings so he goes ahead and enters in Gajendra's cabin. At that time, Gajendra was discussing in a file with his secretary Salila; after seeing Indra, Gajendra asks him to sit down and says his secretary to go outside for a while.

After Salila leaves, Gajendra asks in a low tone-"What happened, did your friend tell you when you can meet The Business God?"

"I met him yesterday."

His eyes become widened, then he asks-"Then, what was the conversation between you and him?"

"He said that he will do our work, but in return he will take Rs. 170 Crores."

"Why, but he takes Rs. 85 Crores from everyone, so why is he asking double from us?"

He replies-"When he is about to ruin someone, he charges double.

It is the principle of his business; what could I do, I was bowed down by seeing such a terrible personality."

Then suddenly intercom rings, Gajendra picks up, then he gets to know by receptionist that a man named Robert want to meet you. Then Gajendra replied that he was busy now and send him after some time; then receptionist says-"Sir, Mr. Robert is saying that you were the one who wanted to meet him and you have said that to meet in fixed time, you need him not he needs you." Anyone can get angry on this, he sudden replies-"Who the hell is he? I don't know any Robert. Tell him, if he wants to meet, just wait."

As soon as Indra hears the word 'Robert', his ears pricked up and quickly he says to Gajendra-"Just hold, Business God has sent this man."

As soon as he heard this, he quickly says to his

receptionist-"Okay okay, let him in, right now."

"But sir, he is going, he will about to reach the lift."

On hearing this, both get up and run toward the lift; opening cabin's door with a jerk, both of them are running toward the elevator. All employees are taken aback, seeing their boss running like this; after all, what is special about that person. Gajendra is fast, he reaches the lift first; and sees a man pressing the elevator button. So by running, he stops that lift and when he saw Robert, he felt for a second that he's seen him somewhere before, but he immediately stops thinking about it and apologizes to Robert for his misbehave. By then Indra also reaches there, and what he saw that he is not a man sent by Business God but he is none other than The Business God. He is the man whom he met yesterday. He steps forward and a word comes out from his mouth-"THE BUSINESS GOD"

Gajendra continues to look at him in surprise that the one he stopped and apologized, is The Business God. Both people are afraid that they hurted The Business God, may they not be doomed; both people again apologize. Then Indra says-"Sorry, but I thought that when I will be in my office, then you will come to meet. So we didn't pay heed."

After that both of them get The Business God inside the cabin with respect and Gajendra tells his secretary not to send anyone in; and then asks The Business God to sit-"Today God is here with us."

Then Indra asks to The Business God-"Why did you have to come?"

"If a person wants to have perfection in his work, then only he should to do that work."

Both understand that their work is less done by their team rather than by The Business God. No one else but The Business God has a mind in bringing the brand named 'The

Business God' to such a height.

Business God asks-"In all these years, first time I get to know about the person, for whom I have to come in front due to curiosity to know about him...

I want to know more about Samrat. When I heard about him, for the first time I felt that someone has come in front of my comparable. On one side, it is I who have always won the war and on another side, there is he who has never lost the war.

This game is going to be great thrill."

Gajendra and Indra are also thinking that due to this reason they have to take help of him.

After a while, The Business God says to Gajendra-"So tell me Rai, how did you meet Samrat and what has been the conversation between you and him?"

Gajendra takes a deep breath and says-"*For a lion, whether the forest is his own or someone else's, he doesn't extend his hand of friendship to another animal of the forest.* But Samrat extended his hand of friendship; he first bought my friendship not because he wants to stand in my good stead but for he can hunt me, like an opportunist.

But sadly, I came to know this late; by then he had squandered my Rs. 70 Crores...

One day, when he and I were drinking together, he told a lot about his past that how he lived his life out of great poverty and now he wants to rob those robber businessmen; he looked in my eyes and told that he will be the richest person of the universe whom the world will worship...

He also told me that he exterminates a put an end to entire existence of the enemy and he steps forward by quashing them."

Then Gajendra feels thirsty and he extends his hand towards the glass of water; that is when his eyes falls on his watch, so he immediately tells Business God-"And yes, also this watch of worth Rs. 80,000 was gifted by him."

Business God suddenly jumps out of his skin on hearing this, and he gestures for both of them to be quiet and gestures to Gajendra to take off his watch and give it to him. He gets bewildered, why did Business God say that? He quietly takes off his watch and gives it to The Business God's hands.

Business God starts examine that watch very closely, and tries to separate its parts. Then he forcefully breaks one of the side chains of the watch, suddenly a small black colored pearl shaped thing falls on the table with a jerk. Everyone understands what that thing is?

Indra and Gajendra jerkily stand up in fear; a palpable sense of fear is on both of their faces. But Business God is in relax posture and smiling picks up that thing, and that thing was Microphone...

"What...Microphone? Did Samrat fit that microphone?"-Tony asked in astonishment.

His grandpa nodded; on hearing this, Tony gives a start-"It means, Samrat was listening to all this; the conversation that has happened between these two till now, Samrat came to know all that?"

"Remember, I already told you that Samrat has a habit of wearing Bluetooth in ear and smart watch in hand...the conversations that used to happen between Gajendra and Indra, he always kept listening."

Showing astonishment, he asks again-"But one minute, if Samrat had known all this before then he should have warned his insiders Kavish and Mahidhar in advance so that those people would not be caught."

"You will get the answer in a while, just listen...

Smiling, Business God is looking at that microphone and says-"Samrat, I already wanted that my voice would reach you and see, you arranged it yourself.

A horrifying way to win the war is to never tell the enemy that you are his real enemy, and then you can win the war very easily. But even more horrifying way is to make the enemy realize with the terror of your name that this time he is encountered with his death.

You may have won many battles, but till date no one has won from his death."

Both Gajendra and Indra are standing and thinking that now Samrat has came to know everything, he must have made a plan to give us own back. Both of them are thinking that nothing can be trusted now; like if he could fit microphone in the watch, he might have fitted microphones somewhere else in the cabin also.

Business God looks at Gajendra Rai who is now trembling with fear and then says to Samrat who is on the other side of microphone-"*The enemy's gift is even more pestilent than his dagger,* perhaps Gajendra forgot this thing but you bear in mind one thing that *those who see the dream of clutching the sun in a fist, become burnt to ashes; and in front of my individuality, your standing is no more than a whit.*

I have heard that you have very appetite for growth, so finishing you, I will end your appetite forever."

After a pause, The Business God warns Samrat-"Samrat, get ready. Now you are going to face 'The Business God'."

Then after that The Business God puts that microphone in that glass of water and those people are only gazing him; both of them were thinking that Samrat was far from the sense of his plan, but in reality he was so close that he was listening even to the heartbeat of both of them.

Business God stands up and moves toward the glass side of the cabin and looking outside-*"Those are only we who cause to demolish our walls which protect us. If you are detrimented, then it will always be your fault."*

Gajendra and Indra still has not been able to get out of this shock that till now our every single line spoken against Samrat was reaching to him. That broken wristwatch of Rs. 80,000 is still on the table but both eyes are on that sinked microphone in the glass.

Business God writes 'THE BUSINESS GOD' on that glass shield with his gloved hands and says-*"There is more excitement in the war when all the paths to return are closed."*

Samrat too is smiling after hearing all this and he also takes off that Bluetooth and put it that into the glass of water. Samrat's strategies were very far-sighted, he was never defeated by anyone nor will he ever defeated by anyone. He started keeping an eye on Gajendra Rai from the very beginning; he was so overwhelmed by the gift given by Samrat and by the stories of his past that he never moved the point of suspicion to that watch. Samrat was laughing at that Gajendra considered Kavish and Mahidhar to messenger of inside news of Homoss Pharma; there is no doubt that they both were insiders of him, but in case of Homoss pharma, Gajendra had kept that matter so secret that it couldn't be leak.

But he had to give Gajendra Rai some reason to bring that inside news to Samrat; that's why he lied to Indra's agent Yati under the influence of alcohol that this news was brought by his insiders and not by some kind of spy microphone, so that his attention will be on all his employees and all the secret information of Gajendra will be kept reaching to Samrat through that watch.

But now there are no insiders nor any watch; therefore, some way has to be found that the every pieces of information about enemy can reach to him.

And for Kavish and Mahidhar, so they will give statement to the police that they have not met me since last one month; so there is no need to worry about them.

Samrat is also thinking that now the real war has started, in which ambush and backlash will arise like the waves of the sea and will also be descend. In these tactics, what looks will not be reality and what is the actual reality will not be seen. But the visionary eyes of Samrat are seeing that no matter how many he got the wounds in midway but in the end, only Samrat will win. And once again he will show the world that Samrat has the power to be in such a top position.

The day of two of these four people ends in awe, but the day of two people is in a kind of pleasure that this time the war is going to be seen by the whole world.

EIGHT

"If you have planned to destroy enemy by attacking his weakness, so on that weakness, you must looking for a time to betray him by showing an ostentatious friendship."

-The Business God

After five days, the annual function of Samrat's firm 'Singh Broking Solutions'...

Big investors and the businessmen of the corporate world have came to this party, in which many people are talking among themselves that the stock market king Gajendra Rai has not came yet. Because in the eyes of the world, Gajendra Rai and Samrat Singh are now friends but the reality is no one knows that these people are sworn enemies of each other.

Another specialty of this party is that both the childhood friends of Samrat, Ayudh and Udatt have also came to it, but yes the world is in illusion that Samrat and Udatt have become friends of each other after the success of Udatt's real estate firm, but everyone is confused why the owner of Alms-givings foundation came to this party.

The function started at 02:00 PM and now it was 05:00 PM; the founder of 'Alms-givings foundation', Ayudh moves toward Samrat. He told everyone whom he met that he had came for donation in his charity foundation by Samrat; and Samrat had drunk a lot. Both know very well that Samrat and Ayudh are not friends yet in the eyes of the world but Samrat has not invite him to this party for friendship to show the world rather has called for enmity, so that in the eyes of the world and Gajendra Rai, they both look enemy of each other and so Gajendra will come in front to establish friendship with Ayudh.And in this way what Samrat wants, it would be done easily; and it happened as planned.

Ayudh goes to Samrat, telling him the specialties of his charity foundation so that any great investor like Samrat donate some money to that foundation. But as he planned, in a drunken state Samrat hits him hard and shouts on Ayudh-"Oh, get lost you bloody beggar." And as the drama was set, he leaves that party in anger.

After some days, according to the plan Ayudh reaches to the Rai Securities Limited and gave a business proposal of the business running behind his foundation.

Gajendra tries to observe him silently and waiting that Ayudh himself broach the matter of squabbling with Samrat. But Ayudh talks only about business. And as soon as he saw a lot of benefit from this social service business, he becomes ready for a huge amount of donation in that foundation.

After when the deal is on, when Ayudh starts leaving, Gajendra stops him and says-"Well, tell me one thing...you must know that I and Samrat are involve in a joint venture insurance. And just a few days ago, there was a small fight between you and Samrat; but still you presented me your business proposal, why?"

Ayudh laughs in his heart because as planned, it was happening; now it was Ayudh's turn to give his best performance in the play, so he brings seriousness to his face and says-"You are his friend, therefore I don't want to express my true feelings in front of you. But let me tell you that by reminding me, you rubbed salt into my wound."

Gajendra cast of mind that today he met with an another enemy of Samrat, if this person come with us, then there will be such a big charity foundation in our support. So he says with the aim of get spewing some more things from Ayudh-"I can understand, *when someone is insulted in a way, it remains a blemish on his credibility for a lifetime.* I'll say him not to do this again in future, he will concede, but...?"

Ayudh says in little anger-"But what?"

"That if he doesn't listen to me then after all what can you do?"

"What can I do?"-he stands up showing his rage. But after a while he again sits and says-"Oh, so you want to spew from me how I am gonna to attack him."

Gajendra started smiling, by then Ayudh says-"Well tried..."-he thumped the table with his hand-"But you can tell this to your friend Samrat that he has added one more enemy to the list of his enemies. Tell him that the owner of the Alms-givings foundation, Ayudh will take revenge for his insult.

Mistakes are often forgiven, but insults are never...

He hurted my ego and I will never forget this. I will definitely take revenge."

Gajendra smirked-"I just wanted to see that anger."-He stands up-"You might not know like the rest of the world, what I wanna tell you...

Me and Samrat are not friends but are bloodthirsty of each other."

Ayudh expresses his disbelief at this point, then Gajendra says again-"You are listening right Ayudh, he is a smirch in the name of friendship. He squandered my Rs. 70 Crores by cheating which by now would have benefited me in billions from the stock market. Partnership with him is just a deal; otherwise I don't like to even see his face.

I, like you, want to see him destroyed. Will you be with us in this, your revenge will also be satisfied."

Ayudh remains silent for a while and then stands up and move towards Gajendra and shakes hand-"Perhaps it is rightly said that the enemy of the enemy is our friend...I'm with you."

Ayudh cast of mind that the thing for which he had came here was successful but Gajendra's feelings will come out so soon, Ayudh didn't expect this; but the same thing is happening as Samrat had said.

Ayudh leaves his office and thinks that at 01:00 AM tonight, he should be very careful about where Samrat called him to meet. Ayudh and Samrat meet at the boundary of an amusement park at that night and deciding their further plans.

But both of them have no idea that these people are being watched, and watching by three men- Indra Singh, Gajendra Rai and The Business God. when by binoculars from a building from afar, these three see Samrat and Ayudh together, then Business God says-"You can see my conjectures, I was right that this Ayudh must be Samrat's man. Such a crooked he is."

Indra says in astonishment-"But Ayudh has been running his foundation for the last ten years, and when did he and Samrat became friend?"

Business God laughs a little then suddenly Gajendra says-"But tell me, how sure were you that Ayudh and Samrat are in one unit?"

Business God replies with a grin-"I was sure that he was going to do some flam in which he would first include a man of his faith in the group of his enemies, so that he can get all our information.

And he was well aware that we would surely be on the lookout for enemies of him. Therefore he showed one of his friends as his enemy in the eyes of the world and then after some time he sent him to you, so that you can make him friend, but he will work only for his friend Samrat." - he laughs out loud-"I like you Samrat...you truly deserve to be called an enemy, I expected this from you..."

But Gajendra is in anger now-"I'll never let off him."

"You are repeating the same mistake you made with Samrat's insiders.

People's relationships are based on the fulfillment of their purpose.

The person whom he has sent to us by making his strength, he will not know when he became his weakness."

Smiling, he looks at Gajendra; and Gajendra has also understood what The Business God wants to say. Both Gajendra and Indra understand that now how to deal with Ayudh. It is becoming such a game, *where pits are being found here on every step but those pits are not to blame, because these are the pits because of which you become expert at jumping.*

The Business God smilingly with his hand, on the glass of building, writes 'THE BUSINESS GOD' and says- *"If you have planned to destroy enemy by attacking his weakness, so on that weakness, you must looking for a time to betray him by showing an ostentatious friendship."*-There is a sly look on the face of The Business God.

Next day;

A car stops at the gate of Singh Broking Solutions, from which a businessman steps out and moves toward the cabin of Samrat; and opening the cabin's door, he asks to Samrat-"Friend, may I come in?"

Samrat beckoned to that businessman and asks him to sit; after sitting, the businessman, asks Samrat for his laptop. Samrat thinks for a while and then he handled that laptop to him. That businessman inserts a pen drive in that laptop and after working for some time, he returns that laptop to him. Samrat and businessman both are smiling and looking at each other but Mr. Datt, standing next to Samrat, does not understand who is he and why he has come for...

After some time, Mr. Datt gets a call and he gets to know that a politician wants to talk with Samrat; when he gave the mobile to Samrat, Samrat is smiling and looking at that businessman. After some time, he disconnected by saying only 'okay'; and then he shakes hand with that businessman.

Then Samrat says to Mr. Datt-"Meet my new friend Parker Nicolson, a diamond merchant from South Africa and he came here to setup his business.

I met him just a few days ago on annual function; he wanted support of any stock market investor of India. So I had lay down a condition that if he can arrange for me 2.01% stakes of Lunar Watch & Company in a very low price from politician Ashwani Gupta, then I'll help him in India. And it was call of that politician, he was very scared and wanted to sell me that shares in very low price."

Then Samrat asks to Parker-"How did you do that?"

"I frightened him, from the world's most dreaded fear, which is called fear of slander.

The fear of slander is a great weakness of a respectable person and whether there is a building or a human being, one attack on his weakness is enough to smash him.

And I did that, of which consequence you seen now. And you have seen how you can control even the biggest rulers."-Parker said.

"I'm impressed man, tell me what you want?"

"Your friendship"

Samrat laughs at this-"Granted, I've given you my friendship.

Now you have no need to fear from anyone in India."

Both are gazing at each other, then Parker said-"By the way, you have such a magnificent and sumptuous cabin, I've never seen such cabin earlier."

"Thanks…Today, after so many years, I've met someone with whom our friendship can last long."

After when this meeting ends, Indra's snooper Yati who was working in Singh Broking Solutions since last one year, she had captured a photo of that person on her phone and reaches Indra's office.

Most of the employees in the office were gone; there were only a few people. When Yati shows that photo to Indra, Indra gets mad; but Yati didn't get the reason for his anger. He tells her to go back and driving his car, he reaches to the Rai Securities Ltd., but he gets to know that Rai left his office for his home. He makes a calls to Rai, then he gets to know that Rai is near City Hospital and moving towards his home. Indra says to him that he has to meet him in the basement of that hospital; even after refusing so much, when Indra forces too much, Rai gets ready to meet with him.

Indra is still very angry and moves toward Rai; and shows that photo to Gajendra. Gajendra too was shocked when he saw that person meets Samrat in that photo because that person was nobody else but The Business God. Both get terribly shocked that now Business God is with Samrat and together they are planning of destroying us.

Gajendra says-"I've said that this person can never be trusted. He doesn't know the difference between loyalty and betrayal. This bloody is among those people that if he see that he can get benefit from his enemy, then he make also him friend."

Then Indra adds-*"Venom will always be venom."*

Both are very furious now, Indra suddenly tries to contact with Business God then he gets reply that he will get the location and time after a few minutes; and they got that after five minutes.

At 08:00 PM, both of them are waiting for The Business God on the terrace of the Classics Hotel; there are more people on that terrace in a short distance away, don't know what they are doing in the terrace even it is evening. Gajendra is thinking how he will talk to The Business God in such a crowd; both of them have their eyes on the roof door that Business God must have about to come on the terrace by walking up the stairs now.

But after a while, there is a voice from behind-"So, why do you want to meet?"

When both of them turn back, they see The Business God in front of them, Business God was already on the terrace and watching them both and now he comes in front.

Before Indra shows his anger, Gajendra stops him and says to The Business God-"Yes, we want to meet you, but see the crowd around, let's us go in secluded place."

Business God laughs-"Don't worry guys; all of them are my men."

Gajendra and Indra turn their gaze around with

amazement, so they now get that all of them are his men engaged in the protection of The Business God.

Gajendra Rai gets a little laugh but Indra cast of mind that The Business God is so vicious, perhaps because of this no police has been able to catch him till date.

Then suddenly Gajendra says-"There is an old saying: -*If one wants to come in power, honesty has to be kept aside.*

You've proven true this saying."

Then Business God asks them both what they are going to talk about; Indra then turns that photo in front of him.

After a while, The Business God smiles-"Hmm...not only I but you guys are also doing something to ruin Samrat...

This is not me but my lookalike."

"Oh...such a kick of made-up story"-Indra satirized.

Business God stops on hearing this and then gestures to a man standing far away on that terrace. Both of them also see that the man ran down the stairs after The Business God's gesture; now why did he ran down, both of them are immersed in that thought. Till then that man comes back to the terrace and stands up in his place.

Till these two turn around and say something to Business God, there is a sound coming from the stairs as if someone is coming towards the terrace.

Both Gajendra and Indra went wonderstruck because he was really a Business God lookalike; they both are repeatedly looking at both with bafflement. Both are in wonder, it means Business God was right; and today the person who met with Samrat was not Business God but was his lookalike.

There is a smile over the face of that lookalike; he

comes near The Business God. Then Business God extends his hand and that lookalike takes out a small pen drive from behind the top button of his coat and gives it to The Business God.

Before they say something, The Business God says-"Tomorrow, I was gonna bring this pen drive to both of you...

This is Bradd; I sent him to Samrat by making a diamond merchant named Parker Nicolson so that he would become his friend and find his weaknesses, he is expert in this."

Temper of both quickly calmed down, and they get that why The Business God is so dangerous and why he never gets caught, because he had appointed his soldiers standing in his protection on every path; who can even give their life to protect The Business God.

Then he again gestures to another person and he immediately takes a laptop and appears in front of The Business God. After when he leaves, he inserts that pen drive into that laptop-*"Either there is friendship or hostility, there must be a reason.*

And that reason was given to Bradd by Samrat in his annual function, in which he did that drama."

That video is on now, which was recorded from the top button of Bradd's coat; and now Gajendra and Indra get relax that Business God has start ruination of Samrat. After that his lookalike returns back to his room.

Then Business God says-*"If your trap is attractive, then your enemies' desires and feelings will not let him see the truth."*

"Yeah...you laid such an attractive trap"-Gajendra said-"Now the days of ruination of Samrat is near."

Till then Indra laughingly deletes all those photos,

and Business God says again-"And remember one thing, Ayudh, Samrat's friend, never gets to know how the real Business God looks like otherwise our all plans will be ruined...

In just a few days, mine lookalike, sensing such weakness of Samrat, and will bring it to me, using which we will able to dance him in our tune."

Then all these three laugh out loud.

NINE

"If a wealthy, capable and powerful man does even wrong things, then it is considered justified; whereas if a poor man does right things, it is considered indecent"

- Samrat Singh 'Sikandar'

After three days;

Samrat has invited Parker for dinner at his house, bantering at dinner; they go to the upper hall and started drinking wine. When they are about to enter that room, Parker says-"You know Samrat, *when we feel that our goal is near, we should move at a double speed.*

I've purchased the property for the showroom with the help of your friend Udatt's real estate firm."

Then pouring out the wine in chalices, Samrat says- "You're right Parker, *in war, the importance of pace can be understood by that warrior who is well aware of the ill-effects of a long battle.*"-He then hands over the chalice of wine to Parker-"*And anyway, if there is no pace in our style, then what's the worth of this life.*"

Both laugh at this because that thing was also right, *if a person takes so much time in making history, then that history itself buried him in the grave of that time.*

Parker cast of mind that today it would be good if anyhow, he gets sense of Samrat's weak link. He slowly starts asking such questions, so that if a little clue is found,

Samrat can be ruined. The recording has already started; he is just waiting for the spewing out the secrets from him. Parker says-"Samrat, I'm impressed by your lifestyle...friend; today, your name is buzzing around all over the India.

How do you feel to hear so many praises?"

Samrat laughs at this-*"The whole world salutes the rising sun but those who want to change the history, they don't worry about praises."*

"Wow...but tell me, what's the reason behind your expensive lifestyle, is this your fondness or your reason to live life?"

"I believe that *if the water is not drawn from the pond from time to time, that water will become muddy.* That's why I would spend money a lot from time to time.

And by the way, if no person has been able to go to heaven with money, then it is better to live life of luxury with that money."-Samrat replied.

"After all, money is such a wonderful thing, isn't it? In a way, the whole world is pursuing only the money..."

"Of course...*the one who has money in his hand, has friends, brothers and kinsfolk with him. The rich person is considered the best person, and thus he spends his life respectfully.*

And let me tell you one more thing, if a wealthy, capable and powerful man does even wrong things, then it is considered justified; whereas if a poor man does right things, it is considered indecent."- Samrat is staring straight ahead with glassy eyes-*"History is witness, the one has ruled the world, who has the largest treasures of wealth. The bitter truth of history that neither has changed yet and nor will ever change."*

Parker came here for something else, but the

personality of Samrat was such that everyone likes him, whether he is friend or enemy. But Parker immediately reminds himself that he has came here to find out the weakness of Samrat, then he is going to ask one question. This time, he hopes that perhaps from this question, he can find out the weak point of him; he asks-"Let you tell me Samrat, who do you love the most in this world, who is your true friend, whom do you trust blindly?"

Samrat again laughs at this, he swigged the wine in a gulp-"My true friend, whom I trust blindly and whom I love the most in this world is nobody else but myself, only myself...I love my life very much.

And not only I but every human in this world loves himself, only himself. In this world, the thing called love is completely over; nobody loves anyone, everybody loves themselves...

Now there is only and only business in this world;everywhere is buying and selling, I am giving this, so I want that in return...only and only business is left in this world..."

Parker thought that maybe if that one might any person, then by dominating him, we can make dance Samrat at our tune.*But the one who loves only oneself can't be dominated, and can't be ruined.*

After a while, when drinking alcohol, suddenly Parker remembers that Business God has told him the specialty of Samrat's secretary that he never left him; if we make join Mr. Datt with ourselves, then perhaps Samrat will become helpless and will be killed in this confrontation. But Parker is now sensed by the style of Samrat that he could be cautious if Parker asked a direct question about Datt, so he beats about the bush-"Dear, tell me, today's businessmen keep a young beautiful girl with them as their secretary, but why have you kept such an old secretary. His memory would also have become weak, remove him..."

There is strong logic behind every deed of Samrat; he answers this question also in well manner-*"The kings of earlier times, they know very well that more than half of the people living in around or in his royal court are of the sycophantic and opportunistic type, and wherever those people see the benefit, they roll away like a temporizer and go there, and when some big trouble comes, first of all those people run away; therefore a wise king always kept some high-grade and high-cultured counselor around him, who never leave the king's side however the trouble is big, that king blindly heed their advices and in his entire kingdom, he used to rely the most on those people.*

Datt is also a devotee of the same type, who is completely devoted to his king. That's why I don't want him to be away from me as long as he has merit...

And this thing, I learned from my father. Earlier, Datt was his secretary; and earlier he was loyal to him, now towards me. He considers me his God."

A flashback reminds and Samrat laughs at some of his past moments that how making emotional fool, he has been taking advantages of his brilliance. Seeing this laugh of his, he asks Samrat the reason for his laughter, then taking a pause, Samrat says-"You know Parker,*if a person is suffering hardship and you help him in his time of sorrow, then he considers you as his God.*

Datt was helped by my father, but I would have taken advantage of him more than my father took advantage of him.

He is simple-minded person, he does exactly what I say, no questions, he has much talent but not a bit of slyness and maybe that's why he doesn't even know how I am extracting his abilities slowly. No doubt, my father has given him very much respect, but I get a lot from him. My father loved him very much but I only pretend to love, after all, he is just a servant, nothing else."-Now Samrat is serious-"My stepfather was as clever as I and also dangerous. I helped him a lot in business, I started love him...But he did one wrong thing."-he now gets angry at his past and he says-"I made him earn so much wealth, made him so rich, his name in the market is only because of me and only me. But don't know from where he got infatuated with his real son Indra, from where he remembered his blood relationship...

I tried him to understand that as I've earned so much money for you, in the same way, I'll take your business and stock firm to a great height; but he couldn't understand it. Don't know how he started remembering his real son and about to give all his property to him by changing his will.

I got very angry; his health was going very bad at that time. I saw the right time, there were only two people in the room- I and Datt. When Datt went out for a while, at that time, I saw the opportunity and then stifle his face with the pillow and that day I killed my father.

What can I do, if I hadn't killed him, I would have had to start all over again. And I didn't want to live that life again, so I was compelled to kill my father, I didn't have any other option..."-Samrat is now silent. But Parker is thinking that after all, what he wanted to know, Samrat spoke out that. Now his last question-"Oh...but suppose if your secretary Datt betrayed you, then what will you do?"

"If the poison spreads in your hand, the only cure for that is to cut off that hand and throw it away."

Next day;

Morning, the founder of Alms-givings foundation, Ayudh came to the Rai Securities Ltd. to meet Gajendra

Rai; Ayudh says–"You said that together we will avenge my insult and your loss from Samrat?

But you neither called me nor gave any message through anyone. Have you forgotten how you were bitten by a snake named Samrat?"

Gajendra knew that Ayudh was actually giving his support to Samrat, but The Business God had said that we do not have to let Ayudh know that we have known his secret. Gajendra is very angry from inside but he has to put false smile on his face–"No, I haven't forgotten at all, that how much harm Samrat has done to me…

I'm not going to forgive him so easily. Rather, I made my first move to ruin him."

"What? Which move?"–Ayudh asked.

"I have bought one senior broker of Samrat's firm, who will give inside information of his firm. Samrat had kept his insiders in my firm, now my one insider is working in his firm; he will expose all the illegal tasks of Samrat.

Now the destiny of Singh Broking Solutions is in my hand…"

Both Gajendra and Ayudh are laughing at this, but there are storms are roaming in the mind of both. Ayudh is thinking that this news will have to be informed to Samrat as soon as possible and Gajendra is thinking that when Ayudh will go and tell all this to Samrat, then surely Samrat will take any wrong step in perturbance due to which Samrat will suffer further.

Ayudh falsely appreciates the plans of Gajendra and thus returns back; as Ayudh leaves from Gajendra's office, Gajendra gets a call from Indra, and Indra says–"The weak link of Samrat is now known and The Business God has called at the same place where Bradd is staying."

Gajendra reaches there early with joy and Indra is

already there, and both of them are now waiting for The Business God. Just then The Business God comes down the stairs from the top terrace with a tablet in his hand.

Business God comes close to these two-*"Feeding a viper with milk only increases its venom, it doesn't become an elixir."*

Gajendra and Indra didn't understand why The Business God said this, they both express wonder; then Business God shows that tablet to them in which that video is on, and in which Samrat is spewing the truth.

As the video was ending, the grin on the faces of Gajendra and Business God kept increasing but Rudra Pratap's real son Indra had a semblance of seriousness on his face. At the end of this video, when Gajendra looks at Indra with happiness, he understood that perhaps Indra is saddened by the fact that Samrat killed his father. Then Gajendra says-"Don't be sad, we will avenge your father's death, now the days of his ruination are drawing near. We have come to know such weakness of him that he will not even know from which side his enemies are attacking him and by the time he would understand, we will have destroyed him."

"I'm not sad about this"-Indra replied.

"So, why is there so much sadness on your face?"-Gajendra expresses his amazement.

He takes a deep breath-"I'm sad that why did I kill my father."

Gajendra Rai and Business God are gazing him with astonishing eyes, then Indra says-"He realized that I was the rightful owner of his empire, he wanted to change his will, but he couldn't change. Would that I had known that he had came to know his real blood."

"But, why are you saying in this that your father died because of you?"-Gajendra asked.

Indra looks at him and says-"I was slow poisoning my father."

Gajendra is shocked and cast of mind that how a son can kill his own father; but this game of money is also great, it can make a man do anything.

Business God is gaping at him and thinking that *history repeats itself over and over again, many times in history, a son has killed his brothers and even his father in the greed of power and empire.*

History is, so that no one makes mistake to repeat it but people learn how that history can be repeated.

The day ends and the night begin;

Ayudh and Samrat meet on the night at 01:00 AM on the same boundary of the amusement park. Ayudh tells him all about how one of his senior brokers is now working for Gajendra, Samrat is smiling even after hearing this. Ayudh says-"Gajendra was saying that the destiny of Singh Broking Solutions is in his hand."

Samrat laughs out loud at this and keep laughing, and then says-"He said that the destiny of my firm is in his hand...

You know Ayudh, *destiny is crueler than it is generous, a bit of the mistake can collide sky with the earth.*

And there was a mistake by him."

Next day, Gajendra gets to know that the owner of Singh Broking Solutions has removed all his senior brokers from his firm because he doubted that one of his senior brokers is an insider.

Gajendra laughs a lot on hearing this; he also tells this good news to Indra that how has his thrown dice do wonders. It happens exactly as The Business God had said; when there is a shortage of brokers in his firm after removing so many brokers, then my insiders will go there as brokers and by and by he will fall into our trap. Samrat feels that the people around him are in control of him but he doesn't know that his friend Ayudh has turned his own cannon towards him. Gajendra says to himself-"Right now I've removed all your extraordinary brokers from your firm. And now I'm going to snatch your secretary Datt from you. It was you who said that the importance of pace in war can only be understood by a warrior who is well aware of the ill-effects of a long battle, so now see our pace that how will we snatch your special man from you today..."

At that night;

Datt reaches his home; he lives alone in his home, a middle-aged citizen, who has only one daughter in the name of family who is living in her 'in-laws' home. He is happy living a life of middle class life; he has not even changed his clothes after returning from office that he hears the doorbell, so he goes and opens the door.

Indra, the real son of his first boss, Rudra Pratap Singh, is at the door; he is sad and his eyes turned red with tears. He looks very dormant and there are tears in his eyes, looks like he just wiped it to hide the tears.

He is surprised that for the first time today Indra has come to his home and too weeping. Datt brings him inside, then Indra says in a wailing-"Someone is with me outside." By then Gajendra Rai, in a serious posture, from behind comes close to Indra and Datt. Datt asks both of them to come inside and to sit.

As Indra sits down, tears well up in his eyes; Datt tries to find out the reason, by then Indra falls on his knees and grabs Datt's hand with both his hand and starts weeping. When Datt asks again, Indra says-"Datt, today

I'm missing my father a lot...my father brought me up very well. He used to bring that thing in front of me even before I desired it. I loved him a lot and he also loved me very much. He fulfilled my every wish, he didn't put any restrictions on me." Indra's throat swells.

Datt's eyes also become moist; it brings a smile on his face when he remembers those precious moments with his boss Rudra Pratap Singh, he says-"I know, I remember all those thing. Those have been such a precious moment in my life that it can never be erased from my mind. My boss loved me as much as you too; he treated me like his younger brother, I can never forget him...

But how did you remember him today?"

"Because today I have came to know the truth about the death of my father, hearing which I am shaken to the core"-he replied in lamentation tone.

"Truth about death, which truth?"

"After hearing that truth, your soul will also tremble from inside."

Then Gajendra gives his mobile to Datt at Indra's behest, and Datt clicks to play that video. As the video is ending, Datt's eyes were widen and red with anger; and after the end of the video, Datt felt like a shock, he sits on the ground taking the support of the couch and the tears start flowing from his eyes. Indra also sits next to him-"Your boss and my father was brutally killed by that Samrat, for whom you are working. Not even once did he think of the favor my father had done for him that how my father made him a millionaire by raising him up from the streets, in return of this he suppressed his mouth with a pillow and brutally killed him."-He cries-"Today I'm missing him a lot...if I had been there at that time, my father would have been alive today."

Datt's eyes are brimmed with tears, he folds his hand-"Forgive me son, I'm your guilty. I was supporting my boss's murderer, leaving the one I should have supported. Don't know how many years of my life are filled with sin, I was living a meaningless life till now.

Your father's last wish was to give everything back to you but that bloody murderer robbed the shield of the father from you. Please forgive me son, I didn't know about this side of him."

"Don't you apologize, you didn't make any mistake, and on the contrary, you supported my father by being with him for so many years. You kept his brand name forever,and you never left him.

The real culprit is Samrat, a treacherous person. Even he is more venomous than a snake, he bitten him who had favored him by adopting. I'll never forgive that ungrateful."-Indra said.

After a while, Indra says to Datt-"Will you be with us in destroying the empire of Samrat, to take revenge of your boss?"

Datt remains silent for some time and gradually, the same anger is coming across on his face which was on Indra's face-"I'm with you, that Samrat had killed my elder brother like boss, now I'll ruin him. My loyalty was with my boss, and he misused my loyalty...

You don't be worry, I'm with you. I'll give resignation tomorrow by hitting him on the face and I'll work for you."

Gajendra and Indra look at each other, because Business God has clearly told that he should remain stay in the firm and support us in destroying him from there, then Indra says-"No, you won't do this."

"But why?"

"When you do this, he will get that we are known

with his hideous secret, then he will become more attentive.

If you want to avenge the death of your boss and my father, you will have to live with him for some days and that information has to be passed on to us, so that we could use it to ruin him.

You are the one who stays so close to Samrat, it's you who gets to know the secret of Samrat's business tactics first. If you support us by standing behind him, it will be easier for us to put a dagger in his back.

Just take care of one thing, he should not even sense that you are supporting us by turning against him and joined us to destroying him."

Datt agrees and wiping his tears, he says angrily-"I understand what I have to do...

He misused my talents, now he'll see what I can do. He has no idea how close he has inadvertently made me, so close that I foresee his every move.

He was saying that I'm not clever but till now where has he seen my cunningness, till now he only used my loyalty."

Then suddenly Gajendra breaks his silence-"Take care of one thing Datt, *the person who can kill even his protector for his own benefit, he can harm anyone for his own benefit. Who doesn't be with his father, he can never be of anyone.*"

Then furious Datt stands up-"If the poison spreads in our hand, then we should cut off that hand and throw it away; he said it but he will throw it then, when he will come to know that the poison has spread in his hand...

But by the time he will get know about it, that poison would have spread all over his body.

He loves his money more than himself and if we take

away all his money from him, then he will also get tormented death."

Then both of them moves from there with Gajendra's car; and after going from there, Indra wipes his tears and then both started laughing that how they fooled Datt by emotional blackmailing. Today both of them got the most important man of Samrat in their favor. Then Gajendra says-*"When the person in front realizes that today he has fallen in his eyes, then it becomes much easier to dominate that person.*

Once he said to me that the only cure of thorns of the way is to keep their nose quashed with shoes but now he doesn't know that we have spread out his whole path with poisonous thorns."

The blaxe of vengeance of Gajendra Rai and Indra towards Samrat is increasing day by day, Bradd the lookalike of The Business God has became a friend of Samrat by becoming a diamond merchant named Parker Nicolson who used to send the secret videos of conversation with him to The Business God, about which Samrat has no idea.

And on the other hand Ayudh, Samrat's childhood friend and owner of Alms-givings foundation, fights with Samrat and befriends Gajendra to avenge that humiliation and secretly conveys Gajendra's next moves to Samrat. But Gajendra, Indra and Business God know about Ayudh from the very beginning, so together they deliberately send such information to Samrat, due to which Samrat is working hard in the wrong direction, and he's not worrying about where he should give the most attention.

Samrat's friend Aryendra Chauhan has kept his insiders Kavish and Mahidhar in his custody, but Gajendra and Indra have not been able to realize that all this is just a drama and in actual Gajendra is supporting Samrat, not them. Gajendra Rai and Indra Singh are also unaware like rest of the world that Aryendra Chauhan is not a patriotic cop but a charlatan.

The Business God, along with Gajendra and Indra, has played many ruses against Samrat, under which some insiders of Gajendra were sent as brokers in Singh Broking Solutions; with the help of Bradd, he came to know his great weakness and through which he has turned his right hand, Mr. Shivraj Datt in his favor. And now The Business God is waiting for his that confidential information which would shake the foundation of Samrat's empire.

And all the brokers of Samrat's firm are astonished by Datt's unpleasant behavior towards Samrat that how did the attitude of loyal Datt change.

But no one knows that Mr. Datt is now with the enemies of Samrat and he has a solid reason behind going against Samrat. Now he is in search of that weak link, after coming into his grasp, even a mountain named Samrat can collapse.

All together is mustering Samrat, misleading him, make turning his attention elsewhere. Samrat is the enemy of humanity in the eyes of his enemy, step-brother, Business God and even his most trusted man; who can do anything for his own benefit, anything means anything.

Here behind every unsympathetic and emotionless face, all kinds of disastrous plans are being made, about which no one even gets sense.

Maybe someone is right, *millions of years have passed since animals became humans, but still the law of the jungle follows. Even today in this ruthless world, in a selfish society, every powerful person lives his life by hunting the weaker than himself. Everyone is trying to evince himself powerful, and between them there is a scene of endless war.*

And the same scenario here as well, the person whom Samrat trusts the most after himself has now turned against him; *and then we have to face more troubles, when we don't even know, who among the people around us has joined our enemies.*

TEN

"Satisfying the selfishness is a dangerous game. When anyone has this doubt that our interest is to be served by him, then it becomes more difficult to dominate him. But when you force your enemies to come to you, he gets the illusions that he is controlling the situation."

- Bradd, the lookalike of Business God

And the day comes which many were eagerly waiting for.

One of Samrat's insiders has given Mr. Datt, the name of the company which is going to go through the roof or going to reduce to dust within a couple of months or so. Mr. Datt had to convey that information to Samrat only, but this time he turned his steering towards Rai Securities Limited and he handed that piece of paper to Gajendra.

Gajendra doesn't understand the first few lines of that paper, when he asks Datt about it, he reveals that it is their code words. In which first line 'BUY' or 'SELL' is written; and the name of the company in the second line, and name of the insider in the third line. Decode that thing from the code word to simple English, he has presented that paper in front of Gajendra. He immediately calls Indra and gives all the information, then Indra rushes to Gajendra's office.

Indra reads that paper-"Sell, 'Kohir Diamonds'...

Doesn't your insider give the reason behind 'BUY' or 'SELL'?"

Datt replied in negation. Then Gajendra says-"Well, we got an amazing tip. Why not, we do short selling? We'll book huge profits..."

Indra nodded-"You're right. And I say, share this tip to all your brokers; if the loss of people in the market will be avoided, then everyone will believe in you."

"But what will we give them the reason?"-Gajendra asked.

"Oh man, tell them anything. Now your name itself has became such a big brand that people will buy and sell whatever you say them...

You're a big brand now, take advantage of it..."

Gajendra becomes gladsome to hear his praise, but then his glances fall on Datt and he goes into deep contemplation for some time. He is thinking that, might that Datt is not deceiving us by taking advantage of our trust. After all, he is indebted to Samrat. So he decided that now we will just keep this tip completely secret. Even if relying on it, we get a little harm to us; but even a speck of mud on the brand is not acceptable-"No, right now we'll not play freely on this tip. This thing should be kept completely secret, should not leak out.

Let's try it this time, will score a lot next time."

Indra also understands why Gajendra said this; and then Indra said that he will be back in a while by making a call. Indra's gestures make Gajendra understand that he is going to inform this to The Business God.

After ten minutes, Indra enters in the cabin and he says in sedate tone-"Buy, top five companies of telecom sector."

"What, I don't understand?"-Gajendra asked.

Indra repeated that and says-"This should be written

and sent to Samrat."

"But why?"-Datt says-"I say that even Samrat should not be allowed to know about this. So he can't make profits."

Indra utters-"We want to destroy Samrat, we have to make Samrat out of wealth and this will happen only if he invests in that stocks which fall sharply so whatever we want will happen easily."

"So are the stocks of the top five companies of the telecom sector going to fall?"-Gajendra asked having a grin on the face.

But Datt does not understand anything that what's going in the minds of these two? Datt is surprised and asks Indra from where he got this information.

Indra and Gajendra started smiling and gazing at each other; then Indra comes close to Datt-"Datt, when I came to know about the murder of my father, I had sought the help of a person to take revenge from Samrat. He promised to help me to destroying Samrat.

He gave me this information that the share price of the top five companies in the telecom sector of India is going to fall."

"And who is that person?"-Datt asks to Indra.

Indra first sees Gajendra for a while and then says to Datt-"The Business God"

Datt retrocedes out of fear, his face turned pale with awe. He leans back and sits on the chair taking the support of table and asks-"The Business God?"

Indra says yes, Gajendra is still smiling; then Datt confirms again-"Is The Business God also involved in this?"

Indra's answer is in firmly affirmation, Datt is still sitting silent because he used to get scared hearing the name of The Business God that may his evil eye not fall in their portfolio. But now he gets to know that he is working indirectly for The Business God-"But he is too dangerous, he cannot be trusted in the slightest.

You guys probably don't know that he can leave our side and go with Samrat anytime and he will never condone us."

Indra and Gajendra also knew very well that by paying more money to The Business God, anyone can do him in his favor so to trust him is to stir up a hornet's nest. They had thought about it in the beginning and after much deliberation, they took this step. But after listening to Datt's words, they were again forced to think seriously on this issue. But now what could they do, the arrow has been shot.

Yes, but we can do one thing that we should heed anything of The Business God only after thinking and understanding it with our prudence. This is the only way we can be safe from the double-edged sword named The Business God.

After that Datt does exactly the same, he writes on a piece of paper to buy shares of top five companies of telecom sector and then reaches to the Singh Broking Solutions.

On seeing Datt, the employees started chuckle in low voice that today again Datt has came late; but don't know, why boss doesn't say anything to him. If they do this arbitrarily, then the whole management will be collapsed. Hearing these things, an employee says to them-*"If there is only one major defect in a man, then it converts many qualities into defects.*

But you have declared him idle, bypassing his loyalty of so many years in a jiffy. Also see that even our boss has came late today, maybe that's why Datt also came late."

Mr. Datt moves towards Samrat's cabin, when he meets Samrat, he hands him that piece of paper.

He was smiling while reading it and he says-"You know Datt, *if anything is the most powerful thing in the world, it is 'time'.*

Whether a person is good or evil, if time favors him, he will rule them all, and if time is against him, the same person would be trampling everyone's underfoot."-Samrat returns that paper back to Datt-"You well known what you have to do."

There, Gajendra Rai and Indra make a plan together to meet Business God and ask what he has planned and after thinking what else, this message has been sent to Samrat by Datt that he should buy shares of five companies in the telecom sector. After all what is running in his mind.

Both of them reach to the terrace of the Classics Hotel and wait for The Business God to meet him. Then suddenly both of them heard a voice, 'The whole world has always been under the feet of God'.

Both people look around them because this line can only be said by The Business God. Then another voice heard, 'If you want to meet me, you have to touch the heights'. When both of them look up, The Business God is sitting on the top terrace of the building.

They both move towards the stairs and reach the topmost terrace and stand behind The Business God. Today The Business God neither wearing his goggles nor Bluetooth in ear and nor expensive gloves in hands. Today he is alone, with no guards; he has a beer bottle in one hand and sipping beer, he is beholding the Mumbai city.

Gajendra Rai is surprised to see all this that maybe he is Bradd, the lookalike of Business God. Indra is about to ask something but suddenly Gajendra stops him by holding his hand, and says-"Bradd, you didn't go office today?"

He remains silent for a while and then after one more sip, he says-"*Satisfying the selfishness is a dangerous game. When anyone has this doubt that our interest is to be served by him, then it becomes more difficult to dominate him. But when you force your enemies to come to you, he gets the illusions that he is controlling the situation.*"

Hearing the voice, both understand that this is not Business God but Bradd, but what is the meaning of his utterance, they didn't get. For whom and why he said this? Both of them staring at each other, with bearing confusion in their eyes, and then Gajendra asked-"We didn't get it."

Bradd started laugh and turning his face towards both of them he says-"People easily get how to harm others, but when someone explains to them something for their benefit, then they don't get that...

By the way, Samrat Singh 'Sikandar', the owner of Singh Broking Solutions wanted to meet the owner of Nicolson Diamond & Co. means Parker Nicolson, in his new office in India, today."

"So, what are you doing here?"-Gajendra and Indra both ask in unison.

Then again after a sip of beer, he says-"Today, Samrat has met 'The Business God' in place of Parker Nicolson."

Gajendra and Indra now start thinking that may Business God doesn't make any deal with him and go against us. He is too dangerous person. If one is con then another one is swindler, and if both of them come together then no power in the world will be able to compete with them.

Don't know why this world creates such dreaded people and put forward them. The whole India knew the godfather of Samrat, who supported him and left such a dangerous lion in the open air that his roar resonates all over the world. But who was that person who made The Business God so great by giving his support that even if is called only 'God', it won't be wrong. If The Business God is so powerful, then surely his godfather would also be such a legendary personality, who invested his money on his intelligence and cleverness; but who is that person, no one knows.

Both are thinking that the existence of Business God is now becoming dangerous in this game. Those people are trying to avoid this for so many days that The Business God and Samrat should not come face to face; but today that incident happened. Let it not happen that these two together start playing with us and we cannot do anything. Because these two are so clever that they will not leave a single evidence to get any clue of their being together.

The three men are silently looking at each other till then the voice of a helicopter is heard. Gajendra and Indra look towards the helicopter but Bradd is still sipping beer and looking them as if he doesn't care about the impendence of Business God. But the rest are both concerned and very worried, and they are just looking the helicopter. That helicopter first moves around the terrace of the hotel and then lands on the helipad.

Two bodyguards descend from the helicopter and then after that The Business God, rich in high-grade personality descends and moves towards these three. Seeing The Business God coming towards them, arranging himself Bradd stands up and puts the beer bottle away from him.

Business God gets closer to these three and commands his guards to leave; after that he also commands Bradd to leave, he only wants to talk with these two businessmen.

When everyone leaves, Indra asks to Business God about that fake tip, then he replies-*"Enemies can be misguided by giving avarice. The more the enemy's avarice increases, the more they can be entrapped.*I did the same thing, used his greed to ruin him. Now he will fall into this trap of ours and when he fall on his face, he'll realize that why the whole world fears in the name of The Business God. Then he'll come to know that whatever The Business God says, he does it.

I warned him that I will end his appetite forever and now the time has came when he will come to know that underestimating the enemy gets such a big punishment."

Then Gajendra thinks for a while and says-"So what you mean is that something is going to happen in the telecom sector which will plunge its share price very much. Am I right?"

Business God replies in affirmation and then Indra asks-"What is gonna happen? Due to which its shareholders are going to suffer?"

"Yes, I also want to know this"-Gajendra asked.

Business god gave a sly look as if he has came to know something which can bring down all the telecom companies-"You guys mean to the ruin of Samrat, I mean to money, so you guys stop worrying about it. This is my job and I know how to do it.

Just wait and watch what I'm gonna do, due to which that person will be devastated.

This time, the whole world will see, how The Business God rules over the entire corporate industry, whatever he wants, only that happens. Business God can make any company King or indigent in a snap, one man reigns all over the businessmen and he is only The Business God. The one who worships this God can live in peace and the one who goes against the will of God; he will crush into the dust."-he started laugh, a laugh that comes at the intention of ruining someone-"Samrat, you call yourself 'Sikandar', perhaps you have forgotten that one day even 'Sikandar' The Great has also crush into this dust."

Indra is glad on hearing this but Gajendra is solemn and silent now, because Gajendra Rai does not intend to harm the layman. He always wished well of the people, he is not such a person to be responsible for any kind of economic crisis in the country. Gajendra Rai believes in earning by doing well to others. He never wanted to harm anyone, so after hearing this, for the first time he has been thinking that may he not go against his principles.

Indra would love to see anyone get harmed in the blaxe of harming Samrat. But Gajendra Rai is not that kind of person, he is thinking that now we have gone so far that it is impossible to go back. But even now, what to do? Then one thing comes to his mind and he is about to ask that what happened between Samrat and him today; so he tries to ask-"Well, tell us what happened between you and..."

Then suddenly Business God refuses that he does not want to talk any more-"I said as much as I had to say;now you guys go and watch the crash of stock market after about 5 weeks and enjoy watching Samrat's pride shattered."

Indra and Gajendra Rai look at each other and decide to leave. Both are coming down from the elevator, Indra is very happy today-"Now it's time to enjoy the game.

He considers himself to be the smartest and most cunning person, now he will come to my foot."

But there is a silence on the lips of Gajendra Rai, he says in that sedate tone-"If it's gonna huge plunge in the telecom sector, then we should also sell all its shares."

"Yes, you are right"-Indra replied-"Sell now and will

buy back when the stock's value drops drastically."-He stops for a while and then says with a foxy smile-"SHORT SELLING...that's why I always used to think that whether the market is going up or down, how Samrat always remains in profit.

He has always been use short selling to make profit in bearish market and I think this is the reason behind of his becoming one of the millionaire stock market investors of India.

Any investor can become rich very quickly by short selling provided he is 100% sure that the stock will go down. He always knew which stocks were going to fall.And that's why there is such a big difference between me and his net worth today whereas the legacy was half divided in both."

Saying this, Indra looks at Gajendra, he shows his affirmation but in that same serious posture. Observing him so quiet, Indra asks-"What happened, why you are so deep? Haven't listened to The Business God?The one who did your loss of Rs. 70 Crores, he too will suffer so much now."

Contracting his eyebrows in displeasure, Gajendra replies-"Do you not care about those people who can come on the streets and wander like pauper due to this market crash?

Think about them..."

He replies in reckless manner-"I only think about myself, it's not on me to take care of the society. And why are you thinking about them, forget it.

Everything we do is like two sides of coin, good for some or bad for some but in the end, everyone gets what they truly deserve.

If those people have to come on the streets and wander like pauper,it will be written in their destiny."

"You're wrong here, the destiny you are talking about is just our vengeance fire in which many such dwelling will be devastated.

We only thought of taking revenge on Samrat; we had no intention of robbing the layman and there was no such plan. So why are we gonna do this so that the general public has to suffer an economic crisis?"-Gajendra answers back to him.

Indra averted his eyes from him, he finds all these things rubbish. He is one of those who only see their benefit; he has nothing to do with anyone else's ruination. In the eyes of Indra, a businessman should not think about all these things. Indra no longer feels like talking to Gajendra but then he thinks that Gajendra has to give a lot of support in this game in future, therefore so now he has to take him along. But he senses that his attention has to be diverted first, then suddenly an idea came across his mind and he says-"Okay, let's talk about this later and find a solution for it. First let me take you somewhere."

"Where?"-Gajendra asked.

Elevator stops at the basement of the hotel and its door opens, Indra says-"Oh c'mon my friend, I wanna show you something."

Gajendra reluctantly goes with him; he takes him to the seashore, which is a dock- Carnac Bunder which is located in Indira Docks, Mumbai Port Trust. Indra takes him towards a transport ship standing aside and climbs on it. Indra does not give the reason, even after repeatedly asking Gajendra Rai, for what intention he has brought him here? Both people climb on it; there is a man about 30 years old who takes care of that ship, whose name is Niranjan. Indra asks him about the ship, then he answered that everything is fine there; then Indra asks him to leave them alone for some time, so his answer was that he is going in the basement of the ship for his lunch. Indra also said him that he will not come until he calls.

Port on one side, and the ocean on three sides; but the ship on which these two are standing is a bit isolated. Indra reaches at the shore of the ship and extends both of his arms-"What a scene! Isn't it?"

He nods in the same serious posture standing back-"Now tell me why have you brought me here?"

He takes a deep breath-"Let me tell you something, this ship is in my name."

"It seems."

"You know, when there was a split between me and that devilish Samrat, there was no mention of this ship. Because it was in my mother's name and she gifted me this ship on my birthday. And earlier from this, my father was happy with something and gifted this ship to my mother; so in this way, this ship was not mentioned anywhere in the will of my father. This was long before Samrat came into our lives."

"So why are you telling me this?"-Gajendra says with peeved.

Smiling Indra comes close to him and places his hand on his shoulder-"Relax, just listen."

"What relax"-Gajendra gets annoyed-"Don't you remember what Business God has said that there will be a huge plunge in stocks of telecom sector, we have to alert everyone.

Crores of rupees of millions of people would be invested in these companies due to which they will be harmed to a great extent. There will be thousands of people whose entire capital will be invested in those companies. And if due to this they become pauper, then we will be responsible for all this, because we are the only people who know about this thing.

Do you even have an idea that if there is a huge fall in this sector, then the entire stock market may crash?Such a fall that will have an effect on us too."

Indra keeps hearing all this with a smile and after a while-"I wanna tell you story of this ship."

"I don't wanna hear anything."

"C'mon my dear, I have brought you here to tell this story."

Indra waits for Gajendra's reply but Gajendra is still quiet, he doesn't give any answer; so after waiting for some time, he starts-"You know, my father started struggle with his sixteen friends. My father and his friends worked together as a team. All those people are still in this world except my father.

My father and all his friends indwell like brothers; they all trusted each other completely. They did a lot of job completely, and the profits that were made in it, all those people used to invest in the stocks suggested by my father because they were sure that my father will give them maximum return. And it had to happen, he had a lot of knowledge about stock market, he was expert in making money from money.

My father often used to say, *money attracts money.*

But this wonderful and memorable journey started with a shipping company and this ship on which we are standing was the first ship of that company.

There are many stories of this ship, one anecdote about buying this ship that how they took lots of debt from market, they took risk and how they managed it, and may more anecdotes.

So I want to tell you one of those stories of this ship."-

Indra again stops for a while and then restarts-"You very well know that there is cut throat competition in the industry. Every company wants to overthrow its competitors, they make every effort for this.Persuade, Purchase, Punish, Exploit the Weakness; in every way, everyone is engaged in a conspiracy to drive back his competitor off the field. And in this fierce battle, every small company like startups, project etc. are like a small infantry soldiers, don't know how many die every moment. It is very common for big companies to destroy small companies in their field;this is because big companies are afraid that those who are behind them today, may not jump and go ahead of them. That's why they often used to destroy small companies.

And exactly it happened with this shipping company; to ruin it, a combatant attacked from behind, because of the constitution and the law, a company avoids attacking from the front, because in such a situation, their reputation also gets threatened. So he uses illegal means to defeat the competitor.

And to destroy our 'Indian Shippers & Co.', the owner of the 'Import & Export Shipping agency', Tej Bahadur Verma attacked.

Tej Bahadur's company had 32 ships; he has monopoly in this field, at that time no other company could survive in this field. Everyone was defeated by that Tej Bahadur and left that field. But no one thought that if someone destroys this monopoly, then he becomes the new and only king in this field. At that time there were four ships in total in our company, of which this was the first ship and they named it 'Victorious Ship'.

So Tej Bahadur did that to ruin the name of our company, he secretly laid some container of RDX in this Victorious Ship, and informed the police that our company does smuggling of RDX. We barely survived, we had to grease many of palms, false evidence and witnesses had to be arranged; after suffering through lot of difficulties, after about five months we got a clean chit.

All the members of the company had understood that the mastermind before it is Tej Bahadur; but we were not sure, the investigation was going on in a secret way, but no solid evidence. Then my father and all his friends decided to take it as minor obstacle and move on towards the goal; which turned out to be the biggest mistake of all of them that these people didn't inflict him properly and it went on to become a canker.

Forgiving Tej Bahadur had its bad consequences, he again conspired to attack all of us that too in a big way.

If you don't punish strictly your enemy, then next time he will attack with more ammunition and it always happens.

Whether it is a battlefield, your competitor or personally any bad habit, if all these are not treated at right time and given the right punishment, so next time they will attack by preparing more extensively, with the intention of not giving up.

So next time, Tej Bahadur secretly put a large number of RDX container in our all ships including Victorious ship; don't know when and how he used to buy those people in his favor, who took care of that ships. And also did secretly partnership with the raiding police team.

It was our luck that one of the policemen was one of the high return earners of my father's stock firm and at the eleventh hour he helped us. My father and all his friends quickly came to all those ships and they tied that RDX container with heavy stones and threw it in the sea; when the raiding team arrived, they got nothing and this time they returned empty handed.

Now everyone had realized that if an animal is as huge as it is, but it can come under control, but an evil person should be killed with a sword held in hand because he never come under control, he has to be ruined.

I remember when my father narrated this to me, he told me that *'If an enemy wants to destroy your credibility and reputation, then before him, you have to destroy your enemy totally by burglar on his reputation, and then stand away and let the world criticize and condemn him."*

The traces of solemnly fall from Gajendra's forehead and the line of curiosity takes its place; Indra is happy to see that Gajendra is paying his attention to his story, he further says-"Then these people decided that Tej Bahadur should be taught a lesson this time and this matter should be ended. He should be punished in such a way that he will remember this blight before ruining anyone else again.

The punishment should be as big as his conceit. The ego of every human being is equal to the wealth earn from sin lying with him. The bigger the pantry of money earned through wrong means, the bigger the effigies of his ego.

Then my father and his friends decided that if Tej Bahadur's wealth is equal to ours, then his ego will be low down for some time. Now in such a short time we didn't have 32 ships to come in equal with him, it was impossible to be owner of 28 ships in such a short time. So everyone decided that if Tej Bahadur will have 4 ships reduced from 32, then he will come in the level."

"What you mean to say?"

Indra smiles-"Tej Bahadur wanted to defame us by using RDX, so in return for this, first we joined hand with pirates and robbed 28 ships of his company in the middle ocen and then blew those up with the RDX bomb, BOOM..."

A grin on the face of him but there is an awe arouse from wonder on Gajendra's face; he is thinking is it right to attack on the source of income of the enemy to just take revenge? Wouldn't it be wrong to kill those people living with him just because of the anger over the enemy? Not knowing how many laborers even the officer's rank would be presented in those 28 ships, destroying their family by killing them all, can it really extinguish the fire of vengeance in the heart?

Gajendra is a good man, even when he was thinking so much about harming common men, then there, hearing about the death of so many innocent people, he started feeling disgusted with Indra's father. But what is the use of venting anger on Indra on this matter, because this incident has happened long ago.

Gajendra is gazing him with those wondering eyes, then Indra again starts-"After this incident, Tej Bahadur Verma came on streets, despite having four ships left with him, he went into debt. His entire ego has been shattered; he promised my father and his friends that he would never harm anyone again. He came to us to ask help so that he could save himself and his family from that too much debt. And an interesting thing was he never came to know that we were the ones who destroyed him and we were the ones who saved him later; the consequence of which is that now your enemy becomes your servant because you helped him in his times of sorrow, then he devotes his life in your name and then one enemy is reduced from the list.

But we also learn something from this, *we should answer tit-for-tat, if someone throws a brick at you then you should respond by throwing a rock so the person will not dare any time in future; if a person makes a snide remark to hurt you, you should retort to cause the person deeper hurt or embarrassment.*

And one more thing, we should never make the mistake of forgiving the enemy. This will become your biggest and also the most dangerous blunder because enemies don't think that you have forgiven him but they understand that you don't have enough power to take revenge on him.

Forgiveness is a good thing, but people appreciate it only when the one who forgives has the same strength and power to destroy the enemy. The luster of courtesy resides in our dagger.

Remember that all the wars which ended in a treaty, those treaties have always been under dominance of powerful bloc, only powerful people have benefited.

If you forgive Samrat today, thinking that you have a generous of heart, you have patience, you show kindness to people, that forgiving is a good quality, then you will definitely repent later, because Samrat will consider it your stupidity and cowardice. He will understand that you do not have the ability and power to take revenge and teach a lesson to your enemies. This is the right time to show your strength to your enemies, to make them realize that you are not one of those cowardly people who don't even know to give the answer even after being beaten repeatedly. *Those who do not know how to take revenge for the atrocities committed on themselves and who do not know how to give a befitting reply to the enemies, their soul is dead.*

Gajendra, this is the time to show the power...

Remember Napoleon Bonaparte, he told that *you have to be merciless to get complete victory.*"

Gajendra has been greatly affected by Indra's words because he is right today, because Samrat is no less than a scoundrel one. He will take this apology as another chance to attack us back. Last time, a loss of Rs. 70 Crores; if he is forgiven, he will return with the intention of causing great harm and that too with great preparation. So it would be better to give him a befitting reply.

This is the Machiavellianism and this is the

Statesmanship.

Indra comes close to him and puts his hand on his right shoulder-"Samrat is not only a threat to us but to the stock investors of entire India, you must have known him so much by now that Samrat can harm anyone to any extent for his own benefit; we are the only people in this world who have came so far to ruin his ego by harming him. If we step back today, this swindler named Samrat will loot the whole of India, and there is no doubt that he will ruin you too and will make a different brand of his name by crush your brand value in the dust.

And then the stock market king's crown will be adorned on a swindler...would this be fair?

Believe that when we are doing harm to him, then other people will also suffer but if we do not drag him out of this ground today, then people will suffer even more, and then no one will be able to save these people from loss. So it's better that we do as Business God said."

Gajendra nodded on this and he gets ready for the chase, thinking that this time some people have to bear the loss, but it is very crucial to teach a lesson to Samrat. If this thug is not stopped here, then his fear will end and he will consider himself the king of all.

If this uncontrolled speeding car is not stopped now, then don't know how many will crushed to death.

Indra sensed that now Gajendra is agreed, but one thing is necessary here that the idea of the good for the layman should not come back across in mind of Gajendra.

The dice have been casted, now everyone is waiting; Gajendra Rai, Indra Singh, Shivraj Datt, Samrat, The Business God, everyone is up against someone in this game, but who will win the game, it will depend on who has played how well.*The name of the winners has always been on everyone's tongue but it is also true that only the loser in the game knows the importance of winning. Losing is not a bad thing, but in sluggishness, laziness and indiscretion, there is no apology for this.*

Exact after 5 weeks;

Indra is sitting in Gajendra's cabin and both the people are discussing that as The Business God says, today 5 weeks have passed. But till now there has no decline in the companies of telecom sector. Both Indra and Gajendra have shorted huge amounts of shares in these companies, now if the share price doesn't fall, then both of them will suffer a lot.

Both people are talking that if that doesn't happen as Business God said, then this arrow of destruction will hit us back.

AIRCEIL's network started working at a slow speed from 12:00 in the afternoon, due to which also a downfall of 6.62% in the price of share before the market closed. And after hearing the terrible sound of The Business God in the evening, it is confirm of Gap Down opening in AIRCEIL Company.

And it happens, it touches lower circuit; and also Sensex and Nifty fall drastically.And seeing this opportunity, Gajendra Rai and Indra Singh have squared off the shares of AIRCEIL, and book huge profit in such a short period.

Here these people are booking profits and the destruction causing The Business God is discussing all over the India; in every newspaper, every news TV channel only The Business God and 'MANDMET Virus' are enouncing.

Many AIRCEIL subscribers ported their number into BSNL; also #sellAirceil is trending around all over the country.

Everyone is also afraid of the warning of Business God; after all, what is mean by his warning that 'This outbreak is not going to stop yet'. All the traders are living life in fear at this time.

And that fear turned into reality when the next day the TATA INDICOM's network also started down in speed. In no time, the shares fell by 15.5%.People are now speculating that this chain will continue, so because of this, shares started falling down of companies like RELIANCE, BHARTI TELE-VENTURES and VODAFONE.

Atmosphere of terror in the whole country, people are afraid to invest money in share market; don't know if The Business God's evil eye again falls on their invested companies.

After a couple of weeks a miracle happened. Techpro AV public ltd. came as an angel and they brought an antivirus that can decrypt viruses made from metamorphic codes, because of which everyone in the market heaved a sigh of relief.

And gradually everyone's life came back on track.

ELEVEN

"When so many coincidences are happening at same time, don't ever think of it as mere series of coincidences but should take it as a sign that you are slowly entrapping in the enemy's plan."

- Shivraj Datt

In the bungalow of Gajendra Rai;

It's 09:30 PM, upper hall at third story, Gajendra Rai, Indra Singh, Mr. Datt and Aryendra Chauhan are all glad today; and not only glad but they are today in the seventh heaven.

Gajendra Rai picks up the bottle of Champagne for the celebration and in four coupes he pours out the Champagne; he turns back with a coupe each in both his hands, and with joy, he says with both hands up-"Friends, congrats on win..."

Everyone is very happy today.

Gajendra moves towards Indra and says-"A drink, in the name of ruination of Samrat." Indra happily holds that coupe.

Gajendra Rai steps a little further towards Datt and extends the coupe-"A drink, in the name of getting Samrat punished for his misdeed." Datt holds that coupe having a grin on face but with the solemnity in eyes.

Then he returns back and picks up that coups and moves toward Aryendra-"And a drink, in the names of the one who will put Samrat behind the bars in the near future."

Everyone smiles at this, then Gajendra says raising his coupe-"And mine drink, in the name of vengeance from Samrat."

"Cheers"-everyone said, raising their coupes; then Gajendra says-"*The potentiality of erection cannot be avowed without destruction*; and we are among those who profited from the destruction and from the erection also money will rain."

"You are right"-Indra smiles-"If had we not been warned by The Business God at the right time, we would have been at a great loss.

Such a wonderful person 'The Business God' is. We never imagined that a virus named MANDMET would be behind the decline in telecom sector.

And I think we have broken the record of profit from short selling. No one would have been able to earn so much profit that too in such a short time."

Smile in on every lip; then Indra says again-"Now, he must be repenting, has very proud of his mind. Sitting on the throne of lucre, he considers himself the Sikandar; now he will realize who is standing in front of him this time...

He always won, but Business God rightly said that this time he will face his death."-He raises his coupe-"So the drink, in the name of Samrat's first defeat."

"And also in the name of his first step towards ruination..."-Mr. Datt says-"He considers himself very clever; but one day, every culprit goes behind the jail, this universe definitely punish him for his sin.

It is said that delight and woe keep coming in the life of every human being, first he suffered, then he got delight and pleasure and now again we will give him pang...

His life started with pain and will end with also pain."-Datt moves toward the window-"Samrat, get ready...

The poison has started dissolving in your body."-and he is just beholding the sky.

Gajendra is thinking that perhaps Datt is completely trustworthy now, then suddenly his eyes fall on Aryendra-"Hey Aryendra, listen to what I called you for.

Just take care, may that SEBI and your ED not hot on our heels."

"Don't worry"-Aryendra says.

"And yes, not also toward The Business God."

Gajendra is not finished his thing that till then Aryendra says-"You don't worry Mr. Rai, you guys are out of my target area. I've enmity with that Samrat...

Most of the scammers and fraudsters I have caught till date were enemies of Samrat and from those I came to know that even Samrat has done a lot of scams. But till date I've not found any evidence against him on the basis of which I can handcuff him.

He's like a challenge for me and his existence is nothing less than a fear for me.

And I have a temperament since childhood, either I have killed the fear or I have killed the intimidator."-Sipping Champagne, Aryendra keeps staring at Indra.

Indra is also looking at him-"Truth is reflecting in your eyes, Aryendra.

You don't worry; soon we will put him behind the bars."

Both Indra and Aryendra are staring at each other having solemnity in eyes. But Aryendra is smiling heartily and cast of mind that, 'these people are seeing truth in my eyes...

But these stupid never understood why I always put behind the bars only enemies of Samrat, but not Samrat.

And soon, I will put them also behind the bars.

Don't know what is happening with my friend, he will surely get huge harm by this downfall. He has refused to have contact with him otherwise; I would have gone and told him that his most loyal secretary Datt had now joined his enemies.' Now he brings semblance of humor-"By the way, in a fit of rage, he threw his laptop out the window."

Both Gajendra and Indra agree on this with a laugh, and Indra says-"Yes, yes, I also heard."

"That's why we are celebrating here"-Gajendra laughs.

Aryendra again says-"Good...

He seems to have forgotten this, *in war only a tranquil warrior wins, not a quick-tempered.*

If we want to win in war, then we have to keep provoking him like this, so that he would get furious and take wrong step and then..."

"We can destroy him"-Gajendra completed his sentence.

Standing by the window, Datt turns back and disagrees-"You know guys, what is the success behind Samrat...

That he is a cold-blooded warrior, it's not that easy to provoke him. He is not going to fall in our trap easily.

I've been working with him for so many years; until Samrat's enemies are thinking of their next move, Samrat has made his move.

He often says, *when so many coincidences are happening at same time, don't ever think of it as mere series of coincidences but should take it as a sign that you are slowly entrapping in the enemy's plan."*

For Gajendra and Indra, Samrat is their arch rival; but inwardly they also admire Samrat's diplomacy.

Datt further says–"First, Business God gave him an open challenge, and after that he got the tip about telecom sector, and then Business God intervened in telecom companies...

After this defeat, he would not sit still. He will thrust his heels to find out why The Business God made only the telecom sector his victim. He must be go crazy now to know how The Business God got that he is now going to make huge investment in the telecom sector."

On hearing this, Gajendra and Indra looked at each other in fear of unknown coming and then they turn their eyes towards Datt; then Datt adds–"Maybe, he can put spies behind me too."

Gajendra and Indra are now seeing him with petrified eyes; quickly Indra says in trepidation–"Then you have to be very careful, Datt. He shouldn't even sense that first you show us that tip. You understand...

If he becomes alert, we will not be able to snare him in our trap. And then...

Neither your revenge will be fulfill nor ours. Are you getting my point?"

Gajendra steps toward Datt–"You're right Datt, he is very clever. Maybe he has already put his agents behind you."

Datt nodded on this.

At that time Aryendra is thinking, a perfect enemy should be such who make impossible to sleep in peace.

Suddenly Gajendra says–"Do one thing, he shouldn't

have the slightest doubt on you, so you have to show yourself like an idol of truth and honesty, no one else should be as loyal and honest as you. Such loyalty that those who doubt you, others begin to doubt on them."- Then he sees Indra-*"Honesty and generosity go a long way in disarm the victim. A step with honesty and truthfulness can cover even a hand stained with blood."*-Then he again says to Datt-"Are you getting, use the truth to gain Samrat's trust.

We'll handle everything else."

Datt agrees and asks to Gajendra-"So what's the next move?"

"Hm...after a few days we're going to meet The Business God.

He is such a mastermind; he will surely make a full proof plan to remind Samrat his level.

First we foment him and then we get him to make a fraud, and when he will about to carry out that fraud, we will implicate him in his fraud. All the evidences will be against him, and then finally our revenge will be satisfied.

Now we are all set, we will do as The Business God says; after all, he gave us such a wonderful present. Now we can trust him that much."

Then Indra says-"Yeah, I've been relying on Business God since day one, it was just you guys who were refusing from trusting him completely. But now whatever he will ask to do, we will obey without any question.

Now it is clear that he is wholly with us, in this war."

Suddenly Datt utters-"Anyway, like the layman, I heard only the voice of The Business God. Introduce me to him."

Gajendra and Indra started looking at each other because they know that once Bradd, the lookalike of The Business God met Samrat, Datt have seen him. And if now take him to The Business God then he will get what our real game is. And if he gets to know the whole game then he will not be trustworthy.

Both of them are thinking that till then Aryendra says-"Oh yes, I also wanna see that soul. After all what is in it that the whole of India was shaken by only his voice."

Before Gajendra say something, Indra says-"Of course, I told him about both of you, then he told you guys to wait for the right time. He will meet you guys at the end of the game...

By the way, I'm very glad today; don't know what is happening with Samrat, because with the breakdown of ego, man also breaks down."

After few days,

It is 03:00 AM, Samrat is in his dream; the pages of the past from when he tried to escape every time, in his dream that past haunts him again and again.

In the dream he is seeing the 15 years old Samrat, who is now in love with a beautiful girl whose name is Shayna. And she lives in a house about 2 km. from Samrat's orphanage and she is also teenager of about 15-16 years old; she belongs to an upper middle class family, whose father is a professor and her mother is a housewife.

There is cricket playground on the back of her house, and the players who came to that ground; their attention is often less on the game but more on the side of Shayna's window. Shayna often comes on her window and make instigate the thirst of love in the heart of those players.

Samrat also went there to play cricket one year ago and was fascinated to see him, on that day another name was added to the list of fans of Shayna; but she didn't even know those who were madly in love with her. But at this age the frenzy of puberty speaks loudly.

Samrat's friend have explained him many times that there is a huge difference of status between him and Shayna, but he was obsessed with love of her, every moment only Shayna is occurring in his mind.

Samrat was practicing cricket for the last one year in the ground of his orphanage, he practiced a lot and he improved his game very much by calling children from far and wide; and only reason behind all these that he will impress Shayna by defeating all the players by playing brilliantly in the ground behind Shayna's home and will propose to her by kneeling and will get his love.

It is 07:00 in the morning, Samrat is rousing both of his friends, Ayudh and Udatt by wagging them, Ayudh says with half-opened eyes-"Is it earthquake?"

"No guys, first you get up."

Then Udatt talks in his sleep-"Now what happens to you?how you got up so early today?"

But Samrat was now rapt in the memories of Shayna that how he would express his love to her today, he has a grin on his face-"C'mon guys let's play cricket."

Ayudh rebukes him in his sleep-"What rubbish...go to sleep now, we'll play in the afternoon."

Then Udatt speaks-"Today, have you got a business idea to earn money from cricket, due to which you got up early and also wakening us?"

"Nope guys, today is Propose day...and today Shayna will propose me"-Samrat says smilingly.

Ayudh again abuses him-"She'll propose? And to you?

But look your status man."

He gets annoyed-"C'mon guys, if she won't, I will."

Making a wry face, Ayudh gets up-"Look brother, she is very rich, she will never love a penurious like you. First she will see money in your pocket...

Today's girls choose their boyfriend with their mind and then start talking lovingly to those boys and when she finds a guy richer than the previous one, she approaches to him."

But only the face of Shayna is roaming in the eyes of Samrat, he is not listening to Ayudh-"True love doesn't see affluences and poverty, true love only sees ethos.

And since I've seen her, I've decided that I'll love her for the rest of my life; and never even look at any other girl."-He then looks both-"You guys will be my business partners in future and partners never leave each other in midstream.

So now you guys get ready quickly, in one hour his father will leave for his work and then she'll come on the back window."-saying this he goes to take a bath.

Then Udatt speaks in his sleep-"C'mon partner, get ready for Mission Samrat's Proposal."

"He even knows, when her father leaves for his work"-Ayudh grumbled.

Ayudh was furious but he would do anything for friendship, everyone is now ready and move towards that cricket ground. In the way, Ayudh says-"Brother, the orphanage in which we live, doesn't get much donation; our pockets are empty and the clothes are also stitched from many places.

Seeing us, she'll make us drive away from afar...why're you bent on insulting yourself today, my brother?"

"Dude, nothing such will happen, I'm ogling her since last year and today it will be done. And when it comes to close, only selfishness sees clothes but not love. In love only the heart should be pure"-Samrat says being in his fascinating dream.

Udatt smiles at this and Ayudh says-"You're now blind in love.

Now you don't understand that even love also exist because of selfishness.

Anyway, I'm your friend, I'm always with you."

All three of them are waiting for Shayna after reaching that ground, now its 09:00 AM and these three are waiting for half an hour, but Shayna is not comes yet. These three are warming up and the crowd of boys is increasing all around. More than half of these are crazy for Shayna; some cycling, some skating and some are doing push-ups at corner of the ground, but everyone's eyes are on that window.

Just then the beautiful nymph-looking Shayna, dressed well, comes to her window, as if cold breeze started blowing through the ears of her lovers, everyone started gazing at her. And Shayna also gives a slight smile to everyone, then they become more happy seeing her smile. The cyclist performs a feat by riding a fast cycle, and the skater jumps and start skating, and the boy doing the push-up starts doing pushups faster; but Samrat, Ayudh and Udatt start seeing her with fascination.

Just then, Udatt awakens Samrat from his daydreams; and Samrat starts moving towards the window like a hypnotized. And just staring at her, Shayna also smiles seeing Samrat; as if for a moment Samrat felt like heaven. Then all the boys standing in the field started looking at Samrat.

Shayna smiles and goes back inside, but Samrat is still seeing that window; Ayudh and Udatt are also glad thinking that probably it is done. Then suddenly someone gives a loud kick to Samrat from behind, Samrat loses his daydream and falls into a pile of dust. For a while Samrat didn't understand what happened after all, his face was covered with dust.

He turns back and sees a handsome 17-18 years old looking boy laughing out loud at him; he is very handsome, fair and tall having a stylish hairstyle, expensive clothes, jacket, expensive wrist watch and a thick gold chain around the neck. Perhaps that was he who kicked him so hard and looking at him, he is laughing too; there are about 20 boys behind that boy that too of the same age.

Ayudh and Udatt are also captured by his henchmen. Samrat stands by adjusting his dress and dusting off his face; he quickly sees toward the window and not finding her there at this time, he takes a sigh of relief. And quickly turns his face and runs to walloping him, as soon as he close to him to retort him, his friends capture Samrat and started thumping him.

Then that well-off boy says-"beat him, he tried to attack on me, perhaps he doesn't know me.

Hit him so much that next time, whenever he could see me afar, run away."

That boy's friends keep on beating Samrat by besieging him, just kicking him by dropping him on the ground, sometimes on his stomach and sometimes on his face. Ayudh and Udatt are screaming louder not to beat him, but those boys are beating him nonstop.

Everyone standing around is watching this silently, no one is coming to help him because there are approx. 20 boys cum goons are with him. Samrat now becomes half-dead and is unable to speak anything.

That boy commands then to leave Ayudh and Udatt, both these run towards Samrat and see his condition; then Ayudh gets very angry and frowning with rage, he moves towards that boy to retort. Then again his goons capture

Ayudh and start thumping him; seeing this Udatt comes forward to rescue Ayudh and to beat those boys but then some boys also hold him and started spurning.

After some time, that boy says-"Leave them both...

You guys don't know me."-Then he points to Samrat-"Take him from here and never dare to come into view here again.

And make understand this boy that he will not even look at Shayna again. She is my girlfriend and she only loves me."

Ayudh and Udatt get that now is not the right time to retaliate, his goons also drive away all the boys from there, and no one even dares to fight with them.

Ayudh and Udatt take Samrat and sit a little far away, Samrat is so beaten that he is not even able to speak something, but however he speaks-"I'll not let off those people, I'll definitely take revenge from those. Those are not aware of power of my mind...

Such a liar was saying that Shayna is his girlfriend. But he didn't know that she was smiling looking at me. You guys saw it; and he was saying that she is in love with him."

Ayudh was now looking back in that direction and he turns back in rage-"For whom will you take revenge?"

"Means, for my Shayna..."-Samrat quickly replies.

"For that girl who loves him who is responsible for your and your friend's condition?"

"Are you mad?"-Disgruntled Samrat replies.

"Look back, she is accepting his proposal."

All three turn back, then Samrat goes bewildered and perplexed as if someone had poured cold water on the fire of love of burning in his heart, and he couldn't able to believe his eyes, Shayna was hugging that boy and looked glad.

Samrat couldn't see all this for long and turns, tears welled up from his eyes; he was not in as much pain till now as it is tormenting now. Whom Samrat wanted with all his heart, and because of whom he had vowed not to even see any other girl except her, that girl is looking happy in someone else's arms today.

Then Ayudh says-"I don't wanna add insult to your injury but were you crazy about this girl who is hungry not for love but for money."

Samrat now understands that *love falls to lot of only the riches. There is only a loud kick in the part of the effete and the indigent. The world loves only those who have money and power in this world. No one belongs to anyone in this world; pairs are made from above, all this is rubbish. In fact, we make relationship only with those from whom our selfishness is fulfilled; as soon as that selfishness is fulfilled, those relationship also breaks up. If you have a thirst for love, first of all you have to become resolute in every facet, only then the world will worship you.*

He is silent but all these things are echoing in his mind, tears in the eyes, his voice is chocked with dejection. And he says with chocked voice-"When I will become rich, I'll buy love, friendship, loyalty with that money...everything is sold in this world and I'll buy everything."

His both friends express their sympathy for him, Udatt says-"Samrat, never doubt on our friendship, we are with you even today and will be always with you."

Samrat looks at him and thinks that these are the two only friends who never compromise on friendship in front of money. Perhaps these are my true friends and I'm sure that as they didn't leave my side today, will never leave in future. When I will become rich, I'll make both of them rich with me. Samrat felt a little proud that in this selfish world at least two are his best friends, he wipes his tears and hug them both-"I'll never break up this friendship."

Then Samrat wakes up, he immediately looks at his clock and it is 03:15 in the night; he messages Ayudh from his mobile that he should come and meet Samrat in his office before 12:00 noon today.

Next day,

At 01:30 in the afternoon, Ayudh reaches the office of Gajendra Rai. Gajendra gets a little shock to see him suddenly and thinking that again he will start his drama that what are the intrigues I've played against Samrat; but I'm feeling pity for him, he is inadvertently slitting the neck of his friend is trying to defend.

There is a sly look on the face of Ayudh;Gajendra tries to guess what will be going on in his mind, but didn't sense.

Ayudh moves slowly towards him and staring intently, then Gajendra asks his secretary to go outside. After Salila leaves, looking Gajendra in his eyes, Ayudh says-*"In the war, the enemy stands in front and the friend, behind the back. An adroit king has to keep his eyes on both of them at that time, otherwise he may lose the war."*

There is peace on Gajendra's face but a storm is brimming over in his mind, such a perturbation arose in Gajendra's mind which is indicating that perhaps the man standing in front of himself has came with the intention of telling the truth.

Ayudh says further-"But you made mistake...many people call you by the name of stock market king, isn't it? But you forgot that *a canny king never fully trusts even his most trusted confidants but you've made the mistake of trusting an unknown person.*

Am I right?"

Gajendra is smiling from inside and cast of mind that therefore we never trusted you and we gave you that information by which Samrat could harm himself.

"What you mean to say...it is enigma to me"-Gajendra says having a calm gesture.

"You shouldn't take enmity with Samrat, you made a blunder. Now he won't let off you, he'll definitely take revenge."

"How did you suddenly start praising Samrat today?"-Gajendra smirked.

"I'm his childhood friend so I very well know his style."

"What?"-Gajendra startled; although Gajendra knew that Ayudh and Samrat are in one team, only for some time they are showing their enmity between them to the world, but this is surprising for him that it is childhood friendship. Gajendra had thought from the very beginning that he should not be allowed to have the slightest clue that he knew everything about Ayudh. And he repeats to him only what he has said himself.

This time again Gajendra doesn't reveal what Ayudh understands that the victory belongs to Samrat and him, not to Gajendra. So that those people can be convinced that Gajendra has started being defensive but in actual, Gajendra is waiting for the right opportunity.

Then Ayudh says-"Yes Mr. Rai, me and Samrat are childhood friend, grew up together, we're not each other's friend but very close friend.

That was a ploy, so that you and the rest of enemies of Samrat understand that we have deep rooted hatred and his enemies take me with them."

Ayudh is still looking Gajendra in his eyes and still smirking, but the traces of calmness are on Gajendra's forehead.

Ayudh further smirked-"Shocked?"

The thought is coming again and again in Gajendra's mind, why not break his confidence by telling that we already knew this thing, but at the same time one thing is also emerging in his mind that this will make Samrat more alert. Then wagging his head, Gajendra says-"But what difference does it make? I won...in spite of all your efforts, I got victory, not your Samrat."

Now Gajendra has a proud smile on his face and the look of a wounded lion on Ayudh's face. Ayudh stops for a while-"Don't start looking at the sky overjoyed, you don't know when the rug can swept out from under your feet."

Gajendra now gets annoyed on this, after all how did Ayudh dare to threaten him that too comes in his office.

Then Ayudh says again-"You've offended a lion, he won't sit still anymore...

He has just taken a few steps back, get ready because now he will pounce even harder."-Then he takes out a letter from his pocket and throws it on the table-"Samrat has sent a warning to you.

That's all for now."-Saying this he turns back to go out.

Gajendra, seeing that letter, thinks in his mind that just waiting for that Samrat to flare up and as soon as he takes any wrong step, I'll entrap him in his own snare.

Ayudh is about to open the door, then Gajendra, sitting in his chair, asks him to stop and says-"Here is just waiting for that your lion to flare up, when that lion comes towards me to smite, this hunter will shoot right in the forehead...now get lost."

With a jolt, he opens the door and leaves.

Gajendra's eyes falls on that letter, he picks up and started read; he has solemnity on his face while reading, but a whirlwind of thoughts is swirling in his mind. *The signature of a real businessman is that he controls his face, not his emotions. A businessman's face is his biggest weapon, on the strength of this, he negotiates many deals in his favor.* Then he is smiling while keeping that paper in his pocket, by then his secretary Salila comes and says-"Sir, an IT professional businessman from Saudi Arabia has an appointment with you, he is on time, can I send him in?"

Gajendra nodded, then his secretary sends him in.

That businessman comes in and gave his introduction to Gajendra; his name was Rizwan Ahmed Davre who came from Riyadh, Saudi Arabia. He operates a small IT company in Riyadh, the capital of Saudi Arabia, and came here to expand his business in India that's why he wants a support of any great businessman of India.

After giving his introduction, he extends his hand to shake hands, but Gajendra's attention is elsewhere, that words of Samrat are echoing in his mind which he has just read. When Gajendra doesn't extend his hand, that businessman looks at his secretary.

"Sir"-Salila speaks to grab the attention.

Gajendra realizes his defocus, but he returns in present and shakes hand with that businessman and asks him to sit-"So, tell me, what I can do for you?"

Then that businessman looks Salila for a while and then says to him-"In the deal that I've brought to you, it is beneficial for both of us, but if you want, you can earn a lot from that deal in a very short time through the stock market."-He again sees his secretary and then says-"But I want this deal to be completely secret."

Gajendra understands that what he means to say, so he asks his secretary go outside for some time.

After Salila leaves, that businessman start telling his business model, but pitching was very bad, boring; Gajendra was sitting in front of him, but his attention was on that letter of Samrat. He is thinking of showing this letter to The Business God as soon as possible and in the same way, send our warning to Samrat as well so that he doesn't make the mistake of thinking of us as cowards.

But whenever there were attacks of MANDMET VIRUS in the servers of AIRCEIL and TATA INDICOM, since then there is no contact with Business God; now until a message comes from the front, further moves can't be made properly. The only thing running in mind is that what will be written in the warning we send, then suddenly that businessman says-"So are you ready to invest in this deal?"

Gajendra again returns in present and says-"No, I've no interest on this...you can go now."

He gets some disappointment and then he goes out from there.

Even after his departure, Gajendra's attention was on what happened today, a feeling was rising deep inside his heart that a similar warning should go to Samrat from our side as well.

Your enemy can be defeated in two ways, either by rupturing his moral-courage and intimidating him that winning is not his thing, or the other way is to make him engrossed in the pride of victory so that he starts lax in preparations by getting over-confident and we can take advantage of that.

Which one of these two ways should be adopted for Samrat, is going on in Gajendra's mind.

Despite his defeat, he is showing that he has not given

up yet but is ready to fight again. Do's and don'ts to get him down on his knees, Gajendra was in dilemma.

Just then he gets a call of Indra and he told Gajendra that many days have passed since that virus attack, so due to subsiding that case, now both of us can meet The Business God. Gajendra thinks, well; now approach The Business God with this letter and then he will tell us what to do next. Indra told him that he has left for hotel and Gajendra should also come to meet him there. Gajendra laughs a little on this, that Samrat sent his letter today, and also today The Business God told that we can meet him.

After a while, Gajendra departures for Classics Hotel; when he was about to park his car, then he saw a luxurious Lexus car coming towards him. When Gajendra's eyes falls on driver, he seem like a well-off person, sharpened on the face, expensive rings and wristwatch in hand, and when he opens his mouth a little, then eyes of the person in front get sparkle with his golden tooth. When that person leaves sitting from his expensive Lexus car, Gajendra thinks for a while that maybe he has seen him somewhere but he can't remember where he saw him. But then leaves this thought and starts thinking back about Samrat.

Gajendra reaches the terrace of hotel and he finds that Indra is involved in conversation with Business God and Indra is looking very happy.

Gajendra gets closer to them and says-"Enemy has strengthened his attention to defeat us."

"Isn't he an enemy, who doesn't try hard to win?"-Business God commented.

Raising his eyebrows, Indra asks him in gesture; then Gajendra says-"He has sent a warning to us that we have to kneel in front of him or else if he gets angry then he'll divest everything from us, our fame, our brand name, our domination even my title of stock market king, and we can't able to do anything."

"How dare he, we squandered his so much money, we've won and sitting there he is threatening that we should kneel before him.

Has he gone mad in losing out his money? He doesn't even understand who is on high and who is underfoot now."-Indra expresses his anger.

Indra didn't even complete by then Gajendra takes out that letter from his coat and extends-"Ayudh had brought this, who is his childhood friend.

Indra is very furious now, his ego is today challenged by his most sworn enemy, he immediately grabs that paper from his hand-"What...childhood friend?"

"Hm...Ayudh himself told me. He came to my office today and he spoke out his truth himself"-Gajendra says.

The Business God stood quiet for so long and just beholding them-"Did you tell him that we already knew his truth?"

Gajendra has a solemnity wag of head-"Nope."

By then Indra has opened the letter and is probably shocked to read the first line. Business God also wants to know what is written in that letter. Indra gave a wonder look to both of them and then starts-*Every victory gives arise to a new provocation,*don't go for celebration after winning a small combat.

This time, luck favored you but never trust this luck; if it is with you today, it can be with me tomorrow, that's why I'm giving you one last chance.

Don't dare to mess with me; you,that silly step-brother Indra and your Business God are all not even equal to half of me. So kneel down and confess your crime in front of the people of India.

Mess with me will be the biggest mistake of your life and if you get wrangled, I'll take away your fame, your prestige, your reputation, your title of stock market king and everything from you.

You'll not even sensate when I'll buy up your trusted people around you. The fort in which you're feeling safe living in it, it will become the bars of the prison soon.

It was just a small combat, but if you dare to stir up a hornet's nest, it will be peril to you."-Then crushing that paper in anger, Indra throws it-"Just look at him...he is giving us last chance."

Having hatchet face, Gajendra says-"He thinks he is a huge dreaded monster, from whom we'll scared and will do as he says.

Full of air, though vanquished."

Business God is still quiet, he had not responded to this yet, seeing Gajendra's rage, he puts his hand on his shoulder-*"Fury suits in heart, not in mind."*-He also looks at Indra as if this line is also for him.

But Indra adds-"Just look at his ego man, we won, we pull of the victory in short selling, we squandered his millions of rupees...and this blatant said that we're not even half of him.

I don't understand what he thinks of himself?"

On hearing him, Business God sees him for a while and then turns his eyes to that crushed letter-"Even after so much time, you guys couldn't understand Samrat."

It is surprising for Gajendra that now what he did mistake to understand Samrat; after all now what's the thing that has escaped from his sight and Samrat is taking advantage of it-"Means?"

Then Business God gives a sly look and says-"We wanna provoke him but now he is making us angry, now if you guys has made any wrong step in anger then whatever he wanted, you guys would have done for him.

It's good that you guys are with me right now.

Just think, despite his loss too much, he is just giving a warning...no, he is not so stupid. If he wanted to attack, and to tell the media about the link between you and me that is The Business God, so he never arrect us by sending just a warning.

Now he wants to irritate us, because he has no evidence against us, so he just wants to annoy us."

Both are listening very cautiously to The Business God and now they get that why Samrat has sent that warning letter so that he can make us turbulent by agitating our conceit.

Both think that it is very good here that Business God like cleaver and cautious person is with us who can ruminates every ploy of the enemy and can thwart of it. Business God is the only person on whom we can fully trust in such times, and no one else.

Then Business God adds-"He has also made an another flam with this small letter, and that is he wants to scare us such that we're afraid to trust the people around us. Because he could probably do you a great deal of harm by buying your trusted men, but in this he could be well-turned only if he didn't let you realize this.

So his purpose behind warning us that you should be afraid to trust the people you rely. He wants to see you living in terror all the time so that you always abide in fear and trouble and he carry this game."

Both rest of them agrees on it and praising the farsightedness of Business God from their hearts. But a thought pop into Indra's mind that whether for these reasons Samrat has sent that letter or he really wants to buy people around us and want to turn them in his favor.

Maybe he can do this, so I've to keep an eye on everyone; Yati has been keeping an eye on Samrat from the very beginning. And since I've included that officer Aryendra in my plan, I've kept my detectives on that too, and so far no flaw has been found of him; and maybe now it is right time to told Gajendra that I've put some agents behind him. And the last is Datt, so will have to keep an eye on that too.

At that time, that thought again flashed in Gajendra's mind that we too should send such a warning to Samrat that we're not afraid of him and he should sit quietly like a coward, otherwise next time we will do more scourges to him. It started popping very much that Gajendra opined- "Why don't we also send him a letter from which he gets furious after reading it and become maniac to subjugate us?"

Business God stares him and tries to read him; Indra likes this idea. Before anyone say something, Business God says-*"The first rule of warfare is, when actually we're going to attack, the enemy should sense that we're not in position to attack, when we're going to use our forces, we should show ourselves dormant in front of enemies, when we are near them, the enemy should seem that we are far away from them and when we are actually far away, they should seem that we are very close to them.*

The enemy should always be kept in a state of perplexity so that he abides in that.

Just look at Samrat, he has enough brains that he shook your mind on his only one letter, now it is our turn to bring down the rampart of his self-confidence."

Gajendra and Indra are gazing at each other because the tactics which Business God just uttered, they've not heard yet, although both of from business family. Indra, despite being royal blood, was so engrossed in his pride that he never learned from his father how to overcome the difficulties in business.Gajendra Rai was also from a business family, but he too had not heard this tactics till now.

Business God further adds-"*Like there are many such animals in the forest which are bigger, clever, agile and more powerful than lion, but what makes the lion the king of the jungle is his confidence and his courage...*

What makes even Samrat stand out are his confidence and his courage, and the additional thing is here that he is cleverer than a wily old fox.

If you guys want to checkmate him, then first of all his confidence and courage have to be defeated...which is a hard nut to crack...but not implausible."

People dislike any kind of superiority and they condemn it and when your enemy is being praised in front of you, then at that time, more anger than your enemy is coming out on that person who is praising him.

Both of them are also getting a little angry towards The Business God but both men appeased themselves by giving them serenity that we should never underestimate our enemy.Anyway, there is no any other option except appeasing themselves.

Then The Business God turns around and goes a little far and takes out a packet of cigarettes from his pocket. And after taking a long draw on his cigarette and then blows rings of smoke high into the sky; and looking at the sky, he asks a question to both of them-"Do you know, why Alexander the 'Great' is called the 'Great'?"

Both started looking each other's faces now and then Gajendra answered-"Because once he was the ruler of 2/3 of the world..."

Business God wagged his head on this and turning back, he moves towards Gajendra-"*He is called the 'Great' because he knew very well the value of 'TIME', that's why he had spread the terror of his name in his enemy's territory at very young age.*"–After one more drag, he says to Gajendra–"When Alexander won a territory, the neighboring territory also became aware that the next attack of Alexander would now be on his territory and out of this fear, he used to start mobilization of the war.

At that time it usually takes a week to prepare for any war but Alexander the Great has got the most supreme status in history because of his pace...the enemy kings would have been under the fallacy that the battle is just a week away but Alexander would have put in an appear at the boundaries of that territory with his army just only after three days and then again a battle would be in his name."–He again puffs that smoke rings into the sky and looks Gajendra in his eyes–"*Alexander never wasted his time in sending warnings.*"

Gajendra is spellbound now, he understands that he was wrong about sending warnings, Indra also gets his point and agrees on this and says–"So that means we have to attack on him, as soon as possible?"

Business God nodded on this without seeing him, and then again Indra asked–"So, what you planned?"

Business god moves towards the parapet and beholding the Mumbai city; both are waiting for his answer. Looking at the sky, he says–"*If the snake's hood comes under the feet, then it should be crushed with double force, if it is left alive showing pity on it, it will immediately stretch its hood and will bite with double venom...*

At the same time, Samrat is like that half-dead snake, if there is even a slightly laxity, then the next defeat can be ours."

Gajendra heartily agrees to this and moves towards him–"I know this too that *an enemy's remnant becomes as dangerous after some time as a spark left in a sheaf of grass.*"–Now Gajendra stands next to The Business God–"But now tell me how to extinguish that spark?"

After a while Business God says-"I've a plan..."

On hearing this, both turn their eyes towards Business God without winking, Indra also moves towards Business God, then suddenly Business God says-"There will be a terrorist attack."

Eyes of both become dazzled, hearing this. Will there really be a terrorist attack? Both are just staring him with shocking eyes, but Business God is quiet.

"What, a terrorist attack?"-Indra asked.

Then Gajendra grilled-"And who will attack?"

Showing unconcerned, Business God says-"Samrat"

They again shocked and thinking that why Samrat would plan to terrorist attack, if he get caught by the police, then they never release him. Even he wants to run away, he will not find any place in country, and he may lose his entire wealth and property but he is not so stupid enough to make such blunder.

Gajendra asked-"We didn't understand? Why Samrat would plan terrorist attack?

He knows its ill-effects very well."

"He has dared to judge me less than himself...he has to bear the bad consequences"-His eyes light up with anger.

"But...why he will do such?"-Indra also asked.

Then Business God started smile and says-"Because we'll make him do such."-He started laugh on this.

But Gajendra and Indra didn't understand his laugh, but they are sensing that maybe Business God will plan that terrorist attack but Samrat will be trapped. After a while Gajendra says-"And how do we get him to do such?"

He then hurled that cigarette from that parapet wall-

"Now listen carefully to what I'm going to say.

I've contact with Lashkar-e-Taiba; many of its agents are active here in Mumbai. They are preparing themselves for retaliation to the situation in the Gujarat and Kashmir regions and I'll ask them to take a deal to Samrat...and in that deal, terrorist need a lot of money to make bombs and if Samrat helps them and sponsors that terrorist attack in India, in return Samrat can book huge profits through short selling from the market crash after the blast.

And I'm sure he won't refuse this golden opportunity.

Maybe first he doubts that he is our man but that agent will assure Samrat that his terrorist organization is independent. Even after all this, if he refuses this deal, that agent will make him realize that there are many more dangerous businessman like him who can invest money in this deal; while militate with Samrat, I've came to understand that he doesn't like someone else's growth.

And as soon as he agrees to this deal, the countdown of his ruination will begin. And then after some time when that terrorist organization will take responsibility for that attack, at the same time, they'll also take the name of Samrat and as soon as they will spell his name, Samrat will behind the bars of the jail...

Indian police will never release him, at any cost. And by then Samrat would have shorted a lot of shares then the police would get another proof against him. And Samrat will never be able to prove himself guiltless throughout his life."

Now both of them realize that why it is common for Business God to make number one any company or to knock it down with a jerk; they don't know how to react on it, but then Gajendra says-"The plan...is great."

"Of course"-Indra asserted.

Gajendra then agrees to go with the plan and Indra

also nodded.

After a week in Samrat's cabin;

The receptionist sends a contractor inside the cabin. He comes in and shakes hands with Samrat; then Samrat asks him to sit.

Today Datt is not in office, the contractor looks around and is fascinated by the glare of the cabin-"You have such a nice cabin."

The smiling face of Samrat allows him to speak ahead of him.

After a while, he says-"First I want to tell you that I'm not any contractor, my name is Sadiq Sheikh. I'm recognized here as a leader of the Indian Mujahideen and I've a very clean image here."

"So...what I do?"-Samrat gibed at this.

That front person started smirk and then says-"Okay, let's come to the point.

I'm secret agent of Lashkar-e-Taiba, and I've been living here for so many years. And now a message has came for me and I've been entrusted with some task."

Samrat is listening to all this with an expressionless face and not reacting.

That agent then says-"And that job is that I've to meet some dangerous business tycoons or high net worth individuals and to convince them that they sponsor in our destructive plan.

Lashkar-e-Taiba wants to an attack on trains of Mumbai, but this time they want to involve some new businessmen in our plan.

That money will be used to buy RDX and Ammonium Nitrate and to make bombs.And let me tell you that many businessmen are already making money with us in these ways.

Our business model is, first we go to great businessmen and they give us their black money, and then we make bombs with that money; and we blast it in any corner of India. Meanwhile, already those businessmen shorted huge amount of stocks and after that blast, when market crashes, they square off those shares and earn huge profits.

Our team got that, whenever the market crashes, there is increase in your net worth so it is clear that you also do short selling and of course through illegal methods...

And that's why I came to here."

Samrat is still quiet and just staring at him.

That agents further adds-"There can be no better use of your black money than this. Just imagine how many times more return you can earn by investing a small amount of black money."

Samrat smirked and then gibes-"And why would I believe these words of yours to be true?"

That agent then takes out an ID card and extends towards him-"This is my card, scan that QR code through VPN and you can visit the website of Lashkar-e-Taiba."

Samrat looks it for a while and then sees toward that agent; he gradually picks up it and read his name. Then quickly he scans the QR code printed on it and everything comes true what he said. There are other things on that site like future terrorist attack, suppliers of explosive materials and all sinister things.

When Samrat visited entire site, he throws his card

towards him and also throws his mobile to the table and says-"But what is the guarantee that you will not be get caught and if you get caught, my name will be not leaked?"

"There is no agreement signed in our business...our business is completely run on words. We are true of our words; we do what we say once.

You have to have full faith in us till then.

There is no guarantee of anything in this world, no one has seen the future but due to uncertain fear, if we divert our attention from our goal so it would be a shame on our manhood."

"By the way, it is very surprising to see that someone from the front is telling that he is a terrorist and there will be a terrorist attack on Mumbai.

Are you not afraid that you will be get caught or should I hand you over to the police? Then your plan would have been ruined."

He says looking Samrat in his eyes-"I'm not one to depend only on luck by being defeated by the fear of failure.

I believe that the more seriously we take the fear of failure, the more perfection will come in our work."

Hearing this, Samrat remembers that night when he drank wine with Gajendra; and Gajendra had also asked like similar question and Samrat was of the opinion on that matter that somewhere this fear of failure helps us to reach our destination.

When this thing comes in his mind, a smile comes across on his face-"You think just like me and perhaps that's why I'm doing this deal on...

And maybe with your help I will be able to take revenge on some of my enemies."

Both shakes hand with each other, but this time

Samrat is completely ignorant of what is going on behind the scenes.

That agent has a hidden secret camera in his dress, which live recording is playing in a tablet. And that tablet is in the hands of The Business God, and standing next to him are Gajendra Rai, Indra Singh and Samrat's secretary Shivraj Datt, and everyone has smile on their wolfish faces.

Gajendra says to Indra-"Congratulation Indra, your brother is about to perish. He has invited his own death."

Indra starts laughing loudly and looks up at the sky-"Samrat, get ready to lick my boot.

Whatever wealth and fame you have earned, only and only I had the right over it; I'll take all that away from you."

Then Datt says-"Well, so soon he will agree to this, hadn't thought of it."

Everyone nodded on this, then Indra moves towards Gajendra and looks him in his eyes-"Now I'll show that dog what is a real businessman.

Now he will realize that to what extent a real businessman can go.

That bloody dog said us that we are not even half of him, now he will know that we are all of his three times."- Then he moves towards Datt-"Datt, now the vengeance for the death of my father will be complete.

Now just understand that a tsunami is about to come...in which Samrat's empire will be sinked, but the treasure of the ocean will be left at our doorstep."

"Of course"

Then Gajendra says-"That bastard said that he will take away my title of stock market king. But he doesn't know what the price has to be paid to become a king.

Now we'll definitely show him his status. His wings

are fluttering a lot; we'll cut off his wings."

Seeing everyone, Business God is smiling having an ambiguous face and he then switches off the tablet and says to everyone-"So exactly after three weeks, on 11 July, there will be attack on Mumbai Western Line. And after some days, Lashkar-e-Taiba will send an email to a news channel, NDTV Profit, in which they'll take the name of Samrat Singh, owner of Singh Broking Solutions.

And then after it...Samrat will be behind the bars.

Your vengeance will be complete."

"Now just waiting for Samrat to short lots of shares"-Gajendra then sees towards Datt-"And we'll get to know about it from Datt."

Datt nodded on this, and then Business God says to Gajendra and Indra-"By the way, if you guys want, then you can also book lots of profit by the market crash, through short selling.

Because it is certain that after three weeks there will be a severe plunge to the stock market. Bear will hit the market hard to bring it down.

A businessman is one who never let go off the opportunity. If you have guts then play the dice..."

Gajendra started gazing at Business God at this, he doesn't react then Indra says-"What are you thinking; he is right, put the pedal to the metal."

"Nothing, was just thinking that after the short of shares, we don't back down, so we have to take this risk very cautiously."

"Oh man, Business God has done so much for us and you are doubting on his work.

Now he had told last time that the share prices of telecom sector will fall, and it became true. He is really worth trusting.

Just short in huge amounts...money will rain."-Indra remarked.

Then Business God comes near to Gajendra and puts his hand on his shoulder-*"Those who have to jump, they jump with their clothes on. Who wants to waste time? Just jump, don't wait. If you jump, perhaps your hand may be break, but if you don't, you'll miss the opportunity."*

This kicked Gajendra and finally he agrees heartedly on this, no one knows whether to come such a big opportunity in life or not.

Everything is set now, just waiting for the climax scene.

TWELVE

"In statesmanship no one is an enemy forever and no one is friend forever, only realization of our selfish interest, sometimes by enmity and sometimes by friendship."

- The Business God

After two weeks,

A Mercedes-Benz E-Class stops at the gate of Rai Securities Limited; everyone's eyes are on that luxury car that who is going to steps out from that. Then a man steps out, whom many have seen earlier, but still many has seen today. Who already have seen him, they very well know that he is a friend of Gajendra Rai and today he arrived with a brand new Mercedes-Benz, and who never knew him before, they now came to know about him.

And this man was none other than Indra Singh, he is now very rich and well-off person. He earns a lot from share market, but this all in only in the eyes of world.

Actually, this all his money comes from shorting the share and he is very sure that market will down, there will be a market crash; and now he uses that money to buy a Mercedes-Benz or a private jet, who's going to stop him.

He enters in the office, and opens the cabin's door-
"Hey Rai..."

He was reading newspaper at that time, he turns towards him and he saw a big smile on Indra's face.

With the shine of money, his face is also shining; expensive clothes, costly bracelet and with a marvelous wrist watch, he is seeing Gajendra.

He welcomes and asks him to sit-"You're very shining...what's going?"

"Hey, you know the actuality, after the short of shares, which money I got, that is only shining"-Indra is on the seventh heaven today.

"Now it will shine even more, just wait to the market crash"-Gajendra also smiles with full heart.

"Yes, just waiting for the market crash...will earn this time as we earned last time, lots of pleasure, and now this time it will rain of money"-He is very excited about the market crash and to earn through short selling, and the biggest joy was to get his half legacy back.

"Yeah, of course"-Gajendra added-"By the way, we have to believe the intellect power of Business God, he is such a magnetic person, and that magnet knows very well how to attract money.

His plan was awesome; first he made that computer virus, and then he made crash the whole telecom sector and then after..."

"Hey, I forgot tell you one thing"-Indra interjects.

"What?"

"That thing is, the decline in the telecom sector was done by The Business God with the intention of not destroying Samrat but with the intention of prospering a businessman"-Indra answered.

"I didn't get it"-There is a tone of amazement in Gajendra's voice.

"I tell you all thing...

That day when Business God called us to plan about the terrorist attack, I reached there five minute earlier and I saw that a man is descending from the stairs of terrace, and I felt that time I've seen him earlier.

He has expensive rings and wrist watch, he was talking over the phone, and that moment I saw his golden tooth. And as soon as he saw me, trying to hide his face from the phone, he went the other way.

When he was hiding his face, then I remembered who he was."

"Who is that person?"-Gajendra also wants to know about that person because he also saw him on that day, when he was parking his car.

"That businessman was, whom picture was in the cover page of Forbes India magazine of last issue"

Gajendra is going to spell his name, till then Indra says-"Yes that was the owner of Techpro AV public limited, Atishay Thakur.

That's the same company which made the antivirus of MANDMET Virus, for which reason they achieve monopoly in their field."

Gajendra astonished on this, because he had not a little sense about this at all, after all why Business God has said to write 'To buy top five companies of telecom sector' in that tip.It means, Business God was making prosper to directly that Atishay Thakur to make his company No. 1.

The Business God carried out his two tasks together so well that the world didn't even know about the real game.

"I've seen him that day, but didn't recognize.

I didn't know till yet that Atishay Thakur was earning more money than us at that time.

Business God must have taken money from him but took double advance from us...

It means he caught two fish with one worm."

"That's why he is called The Business God"-Indra replied.

"I thought at that time that maybe that Techpro AV Company has been really trying to break the codes of particular type of that virus for many years, but it was not reality.

It was contract between The Business God and that Atishay Thakur, that such a virus should be inserted on that servers; which antivirus couldn't be made by any other company except his company. And in this way the trust of all the people should be on his company apart from the rest of the companies"-Gajendra is totally surprised.

"Yes that's it, ever since I saw him, I couldn't believe that Business God was helping him at that time, not us"-Indra rejoinders.

"Oh my goodness,

What a great way to get a monopoly...

An entrepreneur first finds the need of a specific market and then makes a solution, and then earns money by selling that product or service. And by gradually adding values to it, achieves monopoly in his field.

But what The Business God did is that the product was prepared in advance and forced the need of that product in the market, and that too such a terrible need, that as soon as it entered the market, he achieved monopoly.

"Oh, such a deadly mind he got"-Such an astonishment for the first time in Gajendra's voice.

Then Indra adds-"Yeah...the way to do business in the

right way is to provide better service than your competitor, so the company grows better than the competitors.

But Business God did that all the competitors were knocked down completely, then this company reached top itself."

Both are very serious now and Gajendra repeatedly expresses his concern that by following the words of The Business God, we may not make a mistake. Because Business God had hidden some secrets form these people about the fall of telecom sector.

But at the same time these people are also thinking whether he should tell or not tell what his real plans are, but we are getting what we wanted. We want to see Samrat get ruined and this time his fame and name will be definitely ruined.

Now nothing can be done, except to wait for a week because on the seventh day there will be a terrorist attack on Mumbai Western Line, which will make the entire stock market tremble.

After some time, Indra says-"Well, I have to leave now.

Anyway, whatever will happen after seven days. We've taken decisions in the matter of Business God after considering everything very carefully.

Now don't think that we played blind...just wait till the showdown, later you will agree that we are the original gangsters of this game."

Gajendra smiles on this.

After seventh day:

Tuesday, July 11, 2006,

After leaving from office, Gajendra was relaxing in his home. It is 06:30 PM, the phone rings; Gajendra picks up. There is Indra on another side and he told Gajendra to watch news channel.

And then he switches on TV,

A continuation of powerful bombs ripped through a backbone of Mumbai's commuter train system during the evening rush hour, killing nearly 150 people, bringing India's financial capital to a dead stop and resurrecting memories of bloodbaths past.

And another bomb exploded at Matunga Road-Mahim Junction, and we don't know that after how many counts this serial bomb blast will stop. Entire Mumbai is left in shock, everyone is afraid to step out of the house.

The number of injured in the hospital is increasing, and phone network is jammed now, so we are providing tickertapes with information of injured individuals.

And another bomb blasted in Borivali, the death toll is rising at every moment.

Rescue operations are active, a state of high alert is declared in India's major cities; both the airports in Mumbai were placed on high alert.

The western line of the Mumbai Suburban Railway network is now shut down, although some trains will resume service later and security arrangements is now become more stringent.

And just a while earlier, The Prime Minister also held a security meeting at his residence in which Home Minister Shivraj Patil, National Security Advisor M K Narayanan and Home Secretary V K Duggal will attend.

Various senior political figures from India and around the world are condemning the attacks and offered their condolences to those who affected by the bombings.

The local trains, a part of the daily life of Mumbai's millions, seemingly symbolized the city's spirit-temporarily broken and struggling to get back on its feet.

Next day, the newspapers that morning reflected the city's dispiritedness. "Mumbai Attacked" cried the headline of 'The Times of India'. Popular tabloid 'Mumbai Mirror' published a cover photograph of a severely injured victim, titled "Stunned". The newspaper and the television news coverage of the scared off deterred many from stepping out of home that day. The roads and railways were deserted that morning.

Police teams began to record statements, several hundreds of them. Victims in hospitals, witnesses at railway stations, anyone in a position to speak about the previous evening's, was welcome, but barring a few suspicious, investigators had no specific leads to work with on the morning after. Who walked into the crowded railway station and boarded packed trains had simply vanished into thin air.

Then, late that night, there was a significant breakthrough in New Delhi. Aijaz Hussain, arrested earlier that year, informed the Delhi Police that an LeT (Lashkar-e-Taiba) operative who had been working in Mumbai for the past few months was responsible for the blasts.

July 12, 2006;

Gajendra and Indra are drinking wine in Indra's bungalow; where Gajendra says-"Business God has fulfilled his promise.

Yesterday was a black day for Mumbai."

"Hm... *soldiers fight even in battlefield, but the war is won only and only by thinking, whoever won the thinking, the victory belongs to him.*

And this time we've conquered the thinking of

Samrat"-Indra swigged the wine in a gulp.

"You're right; tomorrow the market will open at low...and then after squaring off all shares, we'll go to meet Samrat to make him realize his defeat and our victory."

"Tomorrow my years of dream will come true. That bastard will bow down before me.

And I'll remind him of his real position. I'm the only moon of this sky"-Indra laughs at something-"Now Samrat will realize that it is not a blue moon, but dust on his eyes."

Both laughs at this and enjoying the victory.

After some time Indra gets an SMS, just then Gajendra asks-"By the way, no terrorist organization has claimed responsibility for it so far?"

"You're late in asking question"-Indra smiled, and says-"Just got an SMS...and it is written that a terrorist organization Lashkar-e-Qahhar."

Gajendra gets little wonder because according to the plan, Lashkar-e-Taiba should claim this.

But Indra further reads that SMS-"And written that, an e-mail reportedly Lashkar-e-Qahhar to news channel Aaj Tak claimed the outfit was associated with Al Qaeda and Pakistan-based terrorist organization Lashkar-e-Taiba.

And it stated that it had organized the blasts with its module of 16 people and not 14. It also claimed that all 16 people involved in the blasts are safe.

The blasts, according to the e-mail, were in retaliation to the ground situation in Gujarat and Kashmir and were part of a series of blasts that it had planned on targets that include Mumbai's international airport, Gateway of India, Taj Mahal and Red Fort, among others.

According to reports, intelligence agencies are trying to track the mail and the server..."

"One minute, you didn't take the name of Samrat anywhere in this e-mail?"

"That's what I'm searching for, just one minute..."-Indra read the whole SMS, but he little surprised that as Business God said, there should be the name of Samrat, but it is not so.

He is scrolling and scrolling but he didn't find the name, he says-"There is not his name."

"But it was a deal, how can it be possible? Check it again"-Gajendra asks to him.

"Yes, I read the whole message, but there is not even a clue of his name."

"Is it the uncut e-mail?"

"Don't know that"-Indra shrugged his shoulders.

"Send an SMS to your informer to find out about it"-Gajendra says to Indra.

He sends the message and after a while he says-"Maybe it is possible, that there have been some sudden changes in the plan? But The Business God has cut all the contacts, so he couldn't tell us about the changed plan."

"Hm...but how can he do that? And how will our intension to destroy Samrat will fulfill?"-Gajendra asks in turmoil.

After some thinking, Indra says-"Maybe he made another plan to trap Samrat. He is very clever and I've full faith in him.

Don't be worry, our intention will definitely be fulfilled."

Gajendra thinks for a while and then he says-"Maybe it is possible...it means we have to wait until we meet Business God."

"Yeah...we have to wait, no other option."

"Okay...cheers"-Gajendra said, raising his glass.

Next day, Sensex opened marginally in the red with a loss of 0.09% but went on to end the day with a significant gain of 3%, but anyhow Indra and Gajendra made profit by squaring off those shares just the market was opened.

But they are thinking, when their vengeance will satisfy. So they are waiting for the call of Business God.

And after some days,

A call come to Indra that they can now meet The Business God at that terrace. Indra told this to Gajendra and then both departure for that hotel.

They open the door of terrace and step in; they see that Business God is dragging the cigarette, standing next to the parapet.

They step ahead towards him.

Business God sensed the presence of both of them, so he says-"Come Gajendra, come."

Today there was an inkling of victory in the tone of The Business God, hearing this Indra and Gajendra both become glad.

Then without turning back, The Business God says-"There is no place in this industry for gutter worms like you.This place is only for the emperors and the emperorship only run in the royal blood."

Gajendra didn't understand what he is saying.

"Do you remember something?"-Business God turns back.

"What you want to say?"-Gajendra asks in

incertitude.

Business God is just staring at him and after a while he says-"18 years ago...

A broke youngster had reached a stock investor, who went in search of work and wanted someone to invest money on him and in return he was promising to give huge profit to him.

For this he also fell at the feet of that investor, but that man was in his pride.

He kicked that boy to the ground and then he called his security guard and threw him outside the gate of his office, saying that it is very important to belong to a noble family to do business."

Gajendra is just listening to him and trying to remember such incident.

Business God further says-"Yes, I'm that boy who came to your father in search for my godfather...

And you were also there who was just watching that fuss quietly."

Indra stands silently listening to everything that what is wrong with The Business God today, and what he is talking about.

And now it seems, Gajendra remembered everything so he says-"So, what you want?"

"I anyhow get what I want"-Business God says.

They both remain bewildered as to what Business God now got; which he wanted. Before both of them take some thoughtful decision, The Business God snaps his fingers.

Before they both understand something, four bodyguards of Business God come in terrace by that door and round up them, and they point their gun towards Gajendra and Indra.

They both open-mouthed by seeing such scene, after all why his bodyguards encircled them?

Before Indra says something, and what he sees two people coming down from the top terrace, and then they both get taken aback and wonderstruck; because they were none other than their sworn enemy Samrat Singh with his secretary Shivraj Datt.

"The hunter waits until many animals start hovering over his throw, after then he shoots"-Samrat, coming down the stairs, says.

Indra gave a grimace of wry to Samrat, and both of them are gradually realizing that now both of them are trapped in this game, because Business God makes remind the past in which Gajendra Rai's father insulted him, and being surrounded by his bodyguards and in last the presence of Samrat in that terrace.

All are the signs that now they both get trapped in Business God and Samrat's ploy. The fear that was anticipated for a long time in Gajendra's heart, has seem came true today, Business God and Samrat is now together and turned against them.

Gajendra and Indra look around but they feel themselves as captives, and now they can't even move. Now what should they do, they don't understand anything?

Before they think something, Business God says-"By now you guys must have understood that you are entrapped in our game"-Business God turns-"You guys were presuming till now that this game is going on at your behest, but from the beginning, we were making you guys dance at our tune."

In one corner of Gajendra's mind, there is rage aroused from this deception but in the other corner there is a sense of confusion; because despite him earning a lot of returns from short selling, why is The Business God saying that this game was going on his behest?

And the same feeling is also coming in Indra's mind that however Samrat and Business God were deceiving us together, but we hadn't weakened any wall so that anyone could break into our fort. And there was a probability that Samrat and The Business God could go together against us at any time, but why is Datt smiling?

By then Samrat and his secretary Datt come close to them and Samrat says-"*Powerful people have more appetite for power because they know that only powerful people are given importance and high status in this world.*

My dumb and stupid brother, you too got trapped in the greed of that power.

But would that you had learned something from your father, then you wouldn't have fallen into our trap."

"Who fell? And in which trap?

Now I get enough that you and Business God are together, but it doesn't matter.

That terrorist attack happened in reality and we have earned lot of money through short selling, we haven't lost a single penny.

Perhaps you're misunderstanding that you have won, but the fact is that this time you got away from my revenge, but next time you will definitely trapped." – Indra ripostes.

Samrat and Datt began laugh at this, Gajendra and Indra are in wonder that why Datt is laughing at Indra's words.

By then Business God turns back with a laugh-"Till

now this idiot doesn't even know how in big swamp, these people are entrapped, in which they will only sink."

"Which swamp?"-Gajendra asked.

Seeing each other, Business God and Samrat started smiling. And then Samrat says-"The swamp that we had prepared at the time when you first took the name of Business God in that ruins.

Since then you guys have been getting stuck in that swamp, and now you guys can't get out even if you want."

"When it has unveiled now, so just stop twirling"-Indra flares up in angry and also thinking, how the hell did Smrat know that they first took the name of Business God in any ruins -"And maybe you're twirling these thing because you also know that both of you together could not defeat both of us, and because neither of us had left such a weak link because of which you may defeat us."

Indra is sure that even if he didn't win, he hasn't lost either. But Gajendra is afraid of some uncertain danger.

Samrat again laughs at his step-brother.

"Indra"-Business God moves towards him-"Remember always, when you are standing at the enemy base, talk low.

And I think you're the dumbest pawn of this game. You must have suspected me when we first met and accidently I spoke out 'Son of Godfather' and just then corrected by saying 'I mean Samrat's Godfather Rudra Pratap Singh'."

On hearing this, Indra gets stunned because it means the godfather of Business God is none other than his father.

Then Samrat says on this-"Yes, you got right; Business God's Godfather was none other than our father.

But alas, you were unaware of this. Would that you

had been with your father, you would have known many such things which I know at this time."

Business God and Samrat looks at each other, and then Samrat adds-"About a year after your father adopted me, The Business God came to our office, I've known him since then and this is the reason why he was with me in this game, not with you."

"Which game my brother; you get wrong about something, I told you now that we didn't suffer by the short selling, rather we made profit, so in short we're not get defeated"-Indra replied Samrat, but Gajendra is still silent and listening everything.

Then suddenly Datt speaks out-"Sir, break his illusion now, I'm having pity his situation."

"Datt?"-Indra and Gajendra stunned at his utterance and seeing his behavior.

Datt further says-"Why are your eyes become petrified, Indra?

When you were crying at my door, I knew your whole reality at that time...

Yes Indra, I was also doing drama like you guys at that time.

And perhaps you want to know the reason why I'm standing with Samrat, not with you..."-Datt looks at Samrat with that smirking face-"Samrat had deliberately lied to that Bradd who is a lookalike of Business God, that Samrat had killed his father. But the reality is that when my elder brother cum your father breathed his last, at that moment I and Samrat were present in that room, and when he was moribund, he said to me to never leave the side of Samrat.

But the secret of his death then buried with him, but Samrat had doubts in all likelihood, you have killed him, in the greed of legacy,for yearning of which, you are still blind."

This make Indra's blood run cold, had actually Samrat lied to Bradd? Due to which these people made me speak out the truth, he still can't believe these things.

Then Datt adds-"Yes Indra, at that moment, both of us were present on this terrace...and we heard your deeds with our own ears.

At that turn, I decided that whose side I am.

And after that, I approached to you with that tip and then trembling after hearing the name of The Business God, that all was a mirage, a phantasm...to teach a lesson to a brute like you."

"A mirage...a phantasm..."-Gajendra is benumbed now because he was fully convinced that Datt was with him, every time when Datt and Gajendra have met, every time Gajendra saw the rage in Datt's eyes towards Samrat, but a moderate secretary gave hoax to him.

"Hm...a mirage...a phantasm...and why are you so surprised, is it because I acted better than you?"-At this reply of Datt, Samrat and Business God get laugh.

Then Samrat utters-"Yes, a mirage, like that of Ayudh, with the help of whom, you sent your insiders to my firm...

That all was a mirage so that you never doubt Business God and you guys trust him completely...

And by taking advantage of that trust we hoodwinked you."

Gajendra is still not ready to believe these things.

Samrat steps towards Gajendra, and looks him in his eyes-"These were the things of past.

Now let me tell you your future.

After a while you'll behind the bars for funding this Mumbai train bombings...and then the crown of stock market king will be on my head."

"What rubbish?...I didn't fund any kind of terrorist attack, it was a plan to trap you in this plan, but it doesn't matter, in the next combat you'll kneel before this king"- Gajendra rejoins.

Samrat smirks and sees towards Business God, and then suddenly he fastens his eyes on Gajendra-"Rizwan Ahmad Davre, an IT professional, who came to you with a business proposal, from Saudi Arabia.

Remember...

Let me tell you the reality, in fact, the same guy had sent money to those terrorist in Mumbai through Hawala.

Because we told him to do so...

Yesterday he caught and in a while he'll be in India.

Whether he may take your name or not, but because people in your office have seen him and you talking in a closed room...

So the consequence would be that police will arrest you, in this allegation that by causing the market to crash, you can earn money from short selling, due to this reason, you funded that terrorist attack; and in the greed of money, hundreds of people were put to death.

And you'll never be able to get rid of this charge."

Gajendra's forehead is covered with sweat due to the fear of slander, did that Rizwan Davre send money to those terrorist? Isn't he lying? Because if this happens, then his name and fame will crush to dust in no time and no one in this country will support him.

What should he do now so and how to save himself, because this time he'll not be able to prove his innocence;

because there was a private conversation between him and that person, which has no eye-witness. He has no such evidence so that he could tell the people that they have never met.

Indra is also hassled, that what is this Samrat saying after all. And if he is saying right then no one can save Gajendra from going to jail. Entire India is against those terrorists and if it is leaked, then no businessman will support.

Indra thinks-'It's good that the terror funding guy didn't come to his office, otherwise Indra would have to go to jail instead.'

Now Samrat moves towards to Indra-"And my brother, don't be glad, you're also going to behind the bars in this allegation, because you also did short selling and this world have seen you many time with Gajendra."

"Are you crazy...you will send me to jail...to Indra Singh"-Indra's voice was hardened with mordacious-"I'll acquitted in a trice, don't forget this world have only seen me with Gajendra but the same world has no proof that I'd a hand in funding that terrorism."

"Indra, my brother, you never understood me"-Samrat said with a sardonic smile-"How did you forget that I can never forgive you?

I've never forgiven a single enemy of mine, so how can I forget you.

You know *if enemy has set a trap, so according to the enemy's plan, we should keep getting trapped in it, but as soon as the enemy is sure that now he can sit still...we must quickly dodge him and spoil his whole game.*

Similarly, I also kept falling in the trap of you guys, and as soon as you became carefree, I turned the table..."

Indra felt a surge of anxiety, he is heeding to everything very cautiously.

Then Samrat further says-"Do you know what's going to be printed in the newspaper of tomorrow?...

The explosive material RDX used in the terrorist attack has been found from a ship of dock- Carnac Bunder, Indira Docks, Mumbai Port Trust. And the owner is of that ship, Indra Singh; who is a friend of that person who funded this terrorist attack."

Hearing this, Indra's eyes become upturned, he is not believing on Samrat's words. And his face is covered with sweat, because if it is true, then he also has to go to jail. He thinks about something in panic, and then about to moves towards the door.

He is about to move forward, but suddenly his guards stop him there.

Then Samrat voice obtrudes him-"Hey, where are you going my brother?

What do you think that you can destroy all the evidence of RDX by reaching there...no Indra, not at all.

Rather, the police have raided there, and would have come here at any time."

Indra again wonderstruck by this, after all, how did the police know that he is here. Gajendra and Indra looks at each other with bewilderment and perplexity, what should they both do now?

Now both of them are realizing that both of them are really trapped in such a swamp in which these people will only sink down, and can't get out no matter how hard they try. What they are thinking of as their victory, but in reality it was their defeat. In fact, it was all connivance between Samrat and Business God, in which these people are trapped very badly.

Samrat smirks and again says to Indra-"Now your inheritance is mine too.

Because now you're going to reside in jail"-Samrat started laugh at this, and also Business God and Datt is laughing out loud and started mocking at them-"*The wise treasure their power, but they use the power of enemy to destroy them.*

And so did we, trapped you in your own contrived decoy."

"No, it can't be done...I can never lose, no one can defeat me.

Neither you nor this Business God"-Indra is trying to deny this topicality.

"You're vanquished now, denying reality doesn't change reality.

You are completely ruined now.

And I win this game, only I"-Samrat asserted.

Samrat had said that till then there is a sound of someone coming up from the stairs, all eyes are on that door; the heartbeat of Gajendra and Indra is quicken, isn't the police coming up?

That's when the door opens, and a person steps in, who is Aryendra Chauhan.

For Indra and Gajendra, Aryendra came as a ray of hope; their faces suddenly lit up.

Indra moves forward happily-"It is good that you've come Aryendra, you've come at the perfect time.

Arrest them, he is your enemy, Samrat"-And then Indra points at Business God-"And that is The Business God who put that virus in the servers of telecom companies.

And he has also led to this terrorist attack.

Arrest them all"-Indra said with a haunted face.

This didn't affect Samrat; Business God and Datt is still stand smilingly; then suddenly the brooding and fixed face of Aryendra started deriding.

Everyone started laughing and scoffing at them.

This throws them into a blue funk, Gajendra and Indra's eyes are now terror-stricken by this. Isn't Aryendra with Samrat and Business God?

And their surmise turns into reality when Aryendra avows-"You know Indra, *the worst thing about betrayal, it is never comes from enemies, but the people you trust.*

And I'm not your friend now, and let me tell you one more thing, *any friend that turns into an enemy has been hating since day one.*

Yes Indra, since day one, I'm friend of Samrat and working for him, not for you.

Whatever I am is because of Samrat, so how can I put him behind the bars..."

Now Gajendra and Indra are grasping the whole situation that everyone is against them, nobody was with them, not even one person whom they trust.

Indra is wonderstruck-"But how can it be possible? I myself had put my agents behind you, but then, nothing like this..."

"You're still a step behind us"-Aryendra smiles and looks Samrat-"The one who puts his agent behind everyone knows very well how to avoid the agent behind him."

Gajendra's eyes turned red with anger, in a corner of his mind the anger is emerging from this deception, he wants a lot to say at this time, but he is feeling beleaguered himself, he tries to suppress his anger. For the first time in life such a big deceit has happened to him;but only one reason behind it, he is neither Samrat, nor Business God, nor Datt, nor Aryendra, but the only reason is, he should never trusted anyone, never.

Then The Business God slowly moves to Gajendra and stands in front of him, The Business God is looking Gajendra in his eyes-*"In statesmanship no one is an enemy forever and no one is friend forever, only realization of our selfish interest, sometimes by enmity and sometimes by friendship.*

So the royal blood, how is it feeling?...

I said at that time, I was not born to hear my destiny from anyone but to make my own...

I thought you must have recognized me when you saw me for the first time, but you missed. And made the mistake of trusting me completely, which proved to be the biggest mistake of your life...now you'll avoid trusting anyone for the rest of your life.

You guys would be so stupid, I couldn't even imagine. Don't know how many hints you got, from me or from Bradd.

First, till today no one has been able to contact me so soon but within half of a month, Indra's friend went to him and took my name; people in this world are afraid to take the name of The Business God even more than Illuminati but...doubt didn't arise in both of your mind.

Second, you guys got so lost in the news of falling telecom shares that you didn't even think about it, why I went to meet Samrat that day; but you missed.

And slowly I kept on winning your trust, by threatening Samrat with that spy microphone, then by ascertaining the reality of Ayudh, by making crash the stock market and in last by sending my man Robert to Samrat,who gave information about that terrorist attack.

That all were just chronological manoeuver...in which you slowly got trapped."

The lava of Gajendra's heart spring out in the form of tears, but he doesn't take his eyes off Business God.

Just then, at the behest of Samrat, Aryendra calls the police to the terrace and in a short while some constables along with an inspector come on the terrace.

Then seeing those police officers, Gajendra says, looking into the eyes of The Business God-"I'm leaving now but don't think it the cessation of hostilities.

You've taught me a lot today...*the world is very black, don't expect anything and don't show mercy, and for trust...this world is not worthy.*"

At the behest of Aryendra, the police handcuff Gajendra and Indra; then again Gajendra speaks his last words-"I'll come back...then this confrontation will be done."

The police then take them away, and Indra shrieked-"Samrat, I'll never let off you, I'll take revenge, I'll ruin you Samrat..."

And then that shriek gradually subsides..."

Tony is astounded and spellbound by this story and just staring at his grandfather; but there is a smile on the face of his grandpa and he is beholding the wonder for The Business God emerged in the eyes of Tony.

In that ocean noise, he asks to Tony-"So, what you learnt?"

After being stunned for a while, Tony answered-"*If you want the crown of flowers, all the thorns have to be removed.*"

The Business God inside the grandpa of Tony smiles and then says-"Tony, remember each lesson of this story for a lifetime, it'll be very useful."

Tony nodded but still his mind is on Business God.

Then the phone rings, when he sees, there is Robert.

Then his grandpa asks him for a glass of water, after he leaves, Business God attends the call-"Yes, Robert..."

"Sir, I told him that Business God is ready for his work and he'll meet him soon.

And sir, I'll SMS you all details."

"Good"

"Hm...Sir..."-Robert just keeps quiet for a while, as he wants to say something, but he can't say it.

But Business God sensed his silence and he asks-"What happened, Robert?"

"Nothing just...that businessman was saying, 'God never dies, but maybe The Business God has died'."

Then Robert awaits his reply and finally after a while The Business God says-"Tell him..., the new Business God has arisen."